A LOVE AFFAIR WITH GOD

A LOVE AFFAIR WITH GOD

Finding Freedom & Intimacy in Prayer

C. WELTON GADDY

Foreword by HENRI J. M. NOUWEN

BROADMAN
& HOLMAN
PUBLISHERS

Nashville, Tennessee

Published by:
Broadman & Holman Publishers
Nashville, Tennessee

Design: Steven Boyd

4261-46
0-8054-6146-9

Dewey Decimal Classification: 242
Subject Heading: Prayer
Library of Congress Card Catalog Number: 94-14098

Unless otherwise noted, Scripture quotations are from the New Revised Standard Version of the Bible, copyright © 1989 by the Division of Christian Education of the National Council of Churches of Christ in the United States of America, used by permission, all rights reserved. Other versions used are RSV, Revised Standard Version of the Bible, copyrighted 1946, 1952, © 1971, 1973; and Today's English Version, Old Testament copyright © American Bible Society 1976; New Testament: copyright © American Bible Society 1966, 1971, 1976, used by permission.

Library of Congress Cataloging-in-Publication Data
Gaddy, C. Welton.
    A love affair with God : finding freedom and intimacy in
    prayer / C. Welton Gaddy.
        p.   cm.
    ISBN 0-8054-6146-9
    1. Prayer—Christianity. I. Title
BV215.G33   1995
248.3'2—dc20
94-14098
CIP
99 98 97 96 95 5 4 3 2 1

True, whole prayer is nothing but love.
Augustine

CONTENTS

FOREWORD

It is a great honor for me to write a foreword to this book on prayer. When I first started reading it, I thought, *Well, one more book on prayer.* But when I finished it, I said to myself, *This book is a true gem because Welton Gaddy has found a new—yet very old—language for prayer.*

To use "love affair" as the main metaphor for an intimate relationship with God is as original as it is obvious. However, to develop that metaphor in a theologically sound, psychologically sensitive, and spiritually balanced way is a mark of genius.

A Love Affair with God is undoubtedly one of the most insightful, as well as practical, books on prayer. It satisfies the mind as well as the heart. It is built on a solid biblical perspective, rooted in history, and speaks very directly to the needs of contemporary people.

Personally, this book not only calls me to pray well, but also to love well. Although prayer is its main focus, it opens a rich perspective on the most important question in life: "How do I live in a loving relationship with my neighbors and my God?"

Many of our struggles in life have to do with fear: fear of getting close, fear of asking, fear of going somewhere, fear of staying somewhere, fear of taking a risk, fear of confessing, forgiving, healing, and, yes, fear of loving. These many fears, in their endless variety, prevent us from realizing our deepest self. Fear paralyzes us, isolates us, cripples us, and makes us deaf and mute. Fear finally hardens our heart.

The opposite of fear is love: "Perfect love casts out fear" (1 John 4:18). This book is about the perfect love of God. It is a love that calls us to gradually let go of all fear and to enter in communion with God and community with all people. Thus, by faith becoming fully aware of who we are: daughters and sons of our Father in heaven, sisters and brothers of each other.

I am deeply moved that Welton Gaddy has chosen *communion* as one of his core words to speak about prayer. It is a word that for many people has lost its richness. Still, it is one of the words that, when restored to its full mystical meaning of intimacy with God, can become an inexhaustible well, offering water that takes away all our thirst.

Our hearts yearn for communion, for a deep sense of belonging, for an experience of being ultimately safe, for a divine embrace that expels all our guilt about the past and worries about our future. It is the yearning of our heart to be set free to love God and His people.

I feel very much at home in Welton Gaddy's spiritual vision. The thought that we were loved before our birth, and will be loved after we have died, and thus are held safe in God's eternal embrace is very dear to me. It helps us to think about our short life as an occasion to say yes to God's love and to give that love visibility in our ordinary day-to-day existence.

I am deeply convinced that Welton Gaddy's vision is of immense usefulness because it liberates us from the compulsion to prove that we are lovable, encourages us to be free to live the gift of our belovedness without fear, and enables us to share that gift with others in the same unconditional way that it was given to us. I hope and pray that *A Love Affair with God* will reach many people's hearts.

Henri J.M. Nouwen

&

PREFACE

I have never particularly liked books on prayer, though I have read scores of them. Far too many focus either on rational explanations of how prayer works or on detailed recommendations as to how a person ought to pray.

Frankly, such treatises tend to incite guilt rather than offer substantial help about praying. Readers are left with the impression that if their understanding of prayer differs from that of the author and their practice of prayer fails to conform to the specific directions for prayer outlined in the book, then something must be wrong with them. Scrambling to rid themselves of this guilt and eager to find more meaning in prayer, readers begin to approach prayer mechanically rather than personally, imitating the behavior commended by someone else rather than being themselves as they reach out to God.

I don't like that kind of result or appreciate essays which provoke it. For that reason, I never expected to add to the already massive amount of literature on the subject of prayer.

Why, then, this volume?

In my experience, personally and pastorally, I have found that a recognition of prayer as the conversation (communion) which takes place within a love affair is enabling and inspiring as well as freeing. Seeing God as Lover (or Beloved) can prompt prayerful communications from people who previously never dared speak to God. I am willing to risk one more addition to the mountainous stack of books on prayer already in print only because I am eager for more people, particularly those who resist prayer, to understand prayer as the communion which transpires within a love affair. My hope is that such an understanding will enable people to get on with a life of prayer in which they experience liberty and intimacy.

Not only do I want to convey the image of private prayer as a loving conversation with God, I want to write about prayer conversationally. As I wrote these words, I tried to imagine myself sitting with you over a cup of coffee, talking friend to friend.

Here is a synopsis of what follows. Prayer is communication between two lovers. God loves us like no one else loves us. God's care for us reaches infinite proportions. God's interest in us embraces every aspect of our lives. God desires to hear from us regularly and invites us into a running conversation about our thoughts, needs, and concerns.

So, to speak to God is to engage in an intimate conversation—a highly personal, meaningful endeavor which can hardly be considered a chore to be carried out in strict conformity to a set of rules. When we approach God, we open ourselves to the Ultimate Lover—the One who loved the world enough to offer the gift of Jesus, the One who loves the world enough to make possible the redemption of all people. When we pray to God, we engage in an act of sheer freedom in which everything can be stated straightforwardly and the reality of divine grace can be experienced immediately.

One disclaimer is necessary. I am no expert on prayer, not by a long shot. And I have no interest in telling people how they must pray. What follows in this book are insights about prayer born out of the studies and experiences of an individual who continually struggles with prayer and in prayer. In no sense should the contents of this volume be considered "the final word" of one who has mastered the subject and the practice of prayer. At best, my comments about prayer are the confessions of a pilgrim whose journey into prayer stretches much farther into the future than into the past.

I pray that all who read my words will discover a love-based, grace-laced understanding of prayer—prayer that abounds with the freedom and the experiences of the love affair between God (the Lover) and God's children.

☙

I am desperate for your love, Lord.
Anselm of Canterbury

A CRY FOR HELP

I need help with prayer!" The sound of the voice coming through my telephone receiver was one I did not know, though the urgency within it was unmistakable. A stranger had called me long distance to confess his need for assistance in praying and to ask, "Will you help me?"

Caught off guard, I told the man that I would be glad to try to help but that I was not sure how beneficial I could be to him. He interrupted my comment explaining, "I have read some of your prayers. I want you to tell me how to pray."

Suddenly, images from the past rushed into my consciousness: I saw an elderly woman whom I visited in a hospital. She smiled broadly and spoke excitedly. "I have just witnessed three miracles today!" she exclaimed. Then she told me how she had mastered the practice of prayer to the point that God granted all her requests. It sounded like magic.

Quickly, though, another picture demanded my attention. A young wife sat in my office hardly able to speak because of deep, heaving sobs. Finally, she described to me a deteriorating relationship with her husband and her highly disciplined practice of prayer. She explained in great detail how she followed biblical guidelines in asking God for a restoration of her marital relationship and a resolution of their difficult situation. Then, in desperation, she demanded that I answer her question, "What's wrong with my prayers that causes God not to grant my request?"

A biblically-based picture wedged its way into my thoughts. I could see the disciples gathering around their Lord to hear His response to their impassioned plea, "Teach us to pray."

Though I did not know the man on the other end of the phone, these memories reminded me that I was well acquainted with his spiritual kin—brothers and sisters similarly concerned about prayer. I, too, am a member of that family.

Not quite sure how to continue the conversation, I urged him to be honest with God about his feelings and thoughts, his needs and desires. Once again, the fellow interrupted me. "No. You don't understand," he said with a sense of hopelessness in his voice. "I want you to tell me exactly what to say to God. I want to write down your words and use them as my prayer." I told the caller that I could not form words for him. I urged the man to pray to God in his own words.

The following day, the same man telephoned again. After politely thanking me for our previous discussion, he told me that he still needed help. "I know you can't speak for me. So, I want to describe several different situations to you and then hear what you would say to God in a prayer if you found yourself in each of these sets of circumstances. Speak slowly because I want to write down your words."

"Why are my words so important to you?" I asked, wanting to know the motivation behind this unusual request. "I told you," he responded, "I have read some of your prayers. I believe God hears what you say. I want God to hear and answer my prayers. So, please tell me what to say to God and how to say it."

At this point, I made a mistake. For almost an hour, I talked with the man about how to pray. I yielded to his request and gave him specific words and phrases to use in prayers related to a variety of situations. But I failed to speak with this man about what he needed most—an understanding of the nature of prayer. I talked at length about the structure and vocabulary of prayer. I focused on words and ways of praying. However, the critical issue which went unaddressed was the meaning of prayer. It was like trying to help someone who had never seen a spectacular sunset describe such a sight, or seeking to help a person understand a hymn by repeating the text and ignoring the music.

My error was an honest one. Until that time, my primary thoughts about prayer centered on tangibles—should I say "Thou" or "You"; is it best to sit, kneel, or stand when praying; by what title must I address God; with what words should I conclude my prayer; is my prayer too long or too short? Since that point in my life, my dominant thoughts about prayer have changed. Thanks be to God—and to a few insightful writers and thinkers, as well. With invaluable assistance—some from God and some from other people—I have come to a new understanding of prayer and how to pray. The understanding is only new to me. It is as ancient as the revelation from God in the Bible.

❧

PART ONE

*There is no human being
who will not eventually respond to love.*
John Powell, *Why Am I Afraid to Love?*

SEEKING LOVE

CHAPTER ONE

The love between man and woman
can provide powerful glimpses of sacred vision.
John Welwood, *Journey of the Heart*

A HELPFUL METAPHOR

I can speak of God only by means of inadequate adjectives, incomplete images, and woefully insufficient descriptions drawn from personal experiences, the Bible, and Christian history. What other alternatives are there, though? How else can a finite individual discuss the Infinite Being? What earth-bound imagination can possibly sketch the divine dimensions of the Cosmic Sovereign of creation and redemption? What limited vocabulary can capture even a small insight into the nature of the limitless, incomprehensible Absolute who is God? The words and ways of common life can serve as a means of speaking about the uncommon God and facilitating a better understanding of the divine nature.

Images of God in the Bible

The biblical writers used personal experiences and their own cultural background to help them form images to describe God. Each of these images conveys an important truth about God. But none—not one—captures the entire nature of God, or can be pressed too stringently.

Old Testament Images

The inspired writers of Scripture borrowed images from the world around them in an effort to communicate the nature of God. Thus, they described God as a rock (2 Sam. 22:2; Isa. 32:2); a father (2 Sam. 7:14); a king (Judg. 8:23; Ps. 24); a shepherd (Gen. 49:24; Ps. 23); and a judge (Gen. 18:25; Isa. 33:22). Each of these images contributes to a more comprehensive understanding of God. If too much stress is placed on any of them, however, a misperception of God's nature develops.

God can be counted on—God is as solid as a rock, but is not inanimate. God relates to humanity as a family member, but the relationship between God and people involves far more than bloodlines. God rules the earth, but without a throne—and by mercy rather than by awesome power. God cares for a flock more precious than sheep by means of a love no shepherd could ever match. Certainly, God passes judgments, but God's abiding interest is salvation. God is like a rock, a father, a king, a shepherd, and a judge. But God is far more than any one of these—indeed, God is more than all of these together.

New Testament Images

Jesus, too, spoke of the nature of God and God's rule by means of stories, similes, and analogies. His descriptions of God drew from the imagery of daily life in ancient Galilee. Moreover, Jesus piled metaphor on top of metaphor to help people understand the identity of the Messiah and the redemptive ministry to which God had commissioned Him.

As the incarnation of God, Jesus revealed God's nature through the images He employed to identify Himself. Jesus borrowed Old Testament depictions of God—such as shepherd (John 10:1–14), rock or stone (Mark 12:10), and judge (Matt. 25:32f)—as well as introduced new insights into the nature of God—divine physician (Matt. 9:9–13), bridegroom (Matt. 9:15), bread (John 6:35), light (John 8:12), door (John 10:1–9), and vine (John 15:1–11). Similarly, the early church spoke of the incarnate Christ as judge (2 Tim. 4:1), lamb, (1 Pet. 1:19), mediator (1 Tim. 2:5), high priest (Heb. 4:14), stone (Acts 4:11), bridegroom (Rev. 19:7), and door (Rev. 4:1).

Jesus also used easy-to-understand word pictures when He talked of God's rule. "The kingdom of heaven is like a grain of mustard seed . . . like leaven . . . like treasure hidden in a field . . . like a merchant in search of fine pearls, who, on finding one pearl of great value, went and sold all that he had and bought it . . . like a net," Jesus said (Matt. 13:31–50, RSV). Continuing to speak metaphorically, Jesus identified His disciples—the people of God—as salt, light, and leaven (Matt. 5:11–16; 13:33).

You see, I am in good company when I speak of God only by means of figures of speech, word pictures, images, and analogies. Each one of them is inadequate, I know. But any one of them is better than nothing. Like all of those people of faith who have preceded me, I can best understand spiritual realities by means of tangible images. I can best talk of a relationship with the God beyond me by drawing from the dynamics of interpersonal relations around me.

Such metaphorical talk is helpful as long as I keep in mind that the image is not the reality and that the reality is much more than any image of it can capture. Metaphors aid our understanding of God, but God is greater than the content of any metaphor.

The Metaphor of a Love Affair

With the assistance of figurative language, I have come to a much better understanding of the substance of a personal relationship with God and of the nature of meaningful prayers to God. The metaphor of a love affair proves most helpful to me.

A right relationship with God involves falling madly (or sanely) in love with God and nurturing that love to grow and mature. To pray to God is to speak freely and intimately to God within the security of that loving relationship. The conversations of a love affair comprise the content of prayer.

Using the love affair metaphor to speak of a personal relationship with God strikes some people as odd, if not inappropriate. Unfortunately, many of the most popular depictions of love affairs in the present involve only sleazy relationships ruthlessly forged around immoral judgments, casual sex, and a live-only-for-the-moment philosophy of life. Certainly, the metaphor of such a tainted affair makes no contribution to understanding communion with the God whose very nature consists of fidelity and morality lovingly expressed in judgment and redemption. But popular, perverse images of a love affair do not tell the whole story. Not by a long shot.

Let me be specific. What is a love affair?

Two people fall in love with each other. Sometimes slowly—becoming acquainted with each other over a long period of time, developing a mutual friendship, reluctantly acknowledging an emotional bond, timidly expressing affection, and finally declaring themselves hopelessly in love (though *hopefully* is probably the better adverb). Sometimes rapidly—almost instantaneously, at first sight, sensing great attraction and surges of passion, quickly sharing a mutually experienced infatuation and tug of devotion, and cheerfully committing themselves to one another.

Often, at the beginning of a relationship, one person's feelings of love for the other person far exceed anything the other can offer in response. However, with every passing day, the love between the two people grows stronger, deeper, and more mature. As these individuals speak honestly with each other about their feelings, fears, joys, doubts, expectations, and hopes, trust develops. This trust encourages vulnerability. Both lovers sense that there is nothing that cannot be shared between them. Then, entering the scary realm of vulnerability, the two lovers develop authentic intimacy. Even when they disagree or get angry with each other, they know that their relationship is secure, unthreatened by difficulties, and that each will seek to understand and to respond to the other in love.

Lovers do not need experts to tell them to spend time with each other or talk to each other regularly. As a matter of fact, it seems like that's all either one of them ever wants to do. People in love try to begin and end every day by making contact with each other and talking together about whatever is on their minds. Each lover tries to make the other person happy—through words and actions.

Occasionally, moments come when words fail them. In such situations, lovers sit together in silence sharing trembling emotions, exciting thoughts, profound concerns, and fragile dreams. They enjoy each other's presence and share a quality of communion which cannot be matched by whispers or shouts. The silence between them is not a void—a sign of emptiness—but a place where their spirits meet and their lives touch, a bridge across which their love for each other travels to new depths.

Eventually, lovers know each other so well that either one of them can pretty well anticipate what the other will say, think, or feel in every situation. Such knowledge and intimacy do not shut down conversations between them, however. Rather, the joy of a shared life prompts even more communion. In bad times and good times, with laughter and with tears, lovers articulate the obvious, as well as disclose the mystery of their faith, needs, assurances, and requests.

For me, a love affair provides a helpful metaphor for the nature of prayer. It is a conversation between two lovers. The quality of love between the lovers may not be precisely the same when the relationship begins—my love for God will not equal God's love for me—but the love between the two draws them together, moves them in one accord, and keeps them constantly in touch with each other. The affections, trust, devotion, honesty, intimacy, and freedom which characterize the relationship between lovers characterize the content of an individual's prayers to God. Meaningful prayer looks very much like the ceaseless communion which transpires between two people caught up in a love affair.

The Love Affair Metaphor

In Scripture

I wish I had thought of using the love affair metaphor to describe humanity's relationship to God. But that is not the case. Exactly who used it first, I am not certain. Maybe Hosea, the Old Testament prophet.

The Old Testament. Eight centuries before the birth of Christ, a spokesman for God named Hosea described a troubled love affair in which the fidelity of God stood in sharp contrast to the infidelity of Israel. Hurt erupted. And sometimes anger. But God's love for Israel never wavered, not even when Israel behaved as a harlot. God, the betrayed Lover, steadfastly exhibited mercy and grace by pursuing the beloved and reaching out to assure her that their love affair could continue.

Several other Hebrew prophets used the same imagery in their writings. Isaiah likened Israel's relationship to God to a marriage: "Your Maker is your husband, the LORD of hosts is his name. . . . For the LORD has called you like a wife forsaken and grieved in spirit" (Isa. 54:5–6). After writing of Israel's early devotion to God as the love of a bride (Jer. 2:2) and of the nation's subsequent disobedience to God as adultery (3:1–16), Jeremiah captured the true identity of God as Lover and conveyed the incredible depths of this love: "Return faithless Israel, says the LORD. I will not look on you in anger, for I am merciful. . . . I have loved you with an everlasting love; therefore I have continued my faithfulness to you" (3:12; 31:3).

The New Testament. Throughout Jesus' ministry, He frequently referred to God in terms of love, speaking of God's love for the world and every person in it (John 3:16). The tenderness and all-embracing concern of a love affair can be seen as Jesus describes God's sensitivity to a fallen sparrow and awareness of the number of hairs on each individual's head (Luke 12:7).

The apostle Paul chose the image of a love affair to describe the relationship between Jesus and the church. In the love song which appears in Ephesians 5, a passage one commentator entitles "The Romance of Christ and the Church,"[1] Paul identifies Christ as the loving Bridegroom and the church as Christ's beloved Bride. It all starts with God—God's love for the world becomes a means of describing the love which exists between a husband and wife. Then, that marital love becomes a metaphor for the relationship between Christ and the church.

In Other Christian Literature

Throughout the history of the Christian church, love affair imagery has been used to describe the relationship which should (and can) exist between God and an individual. At times, love affair language has been appropriated in the prayers of Christian leaders. For example, John Climacus, a devout man who lived in the sixth century and was often called a saint, addressed God in this manner, "You have wounded my heart, O love." More recently, Madame Guyon of France employed virtually the same terminology, "O my love, it is enough . . . I desire the love which sends ineffable shudders through the soul."[2] The great Baptist preacher Charles Hadden Spurgeon took his favorite name for God from the Old Testament's Song of Solomon—"My Well Beloved."[3]

Several contemporary religious authors write of God as Lover and describe the communion which transpires between people and God as the substance of a love affair. The widely read Dutch theologian, Henri Nouwen, asserts that "Real prayer comes from the heart."[4] When we pray, according to Nouwen, "we descend with the mind into the heart" and thus "enter through our heart into the heart of God, who embraces all history with His eternally creative and recreative love."[5]

After an examination of the variety of metaphors used in speaking about God, Andrew Greeley, a Roman Catholic priest, concludes that the love metaphor is the "'privileged' metaphor, one that takes over and dominates all the rest."[6] Greeley prayerfully confesses to God, "I am overwhelmed . . . almost to the point of tears, by the picture of You as the vulnerable lover, fragile in the face of the freedom You have given us."[7] Not surprisingly, Greeley frequently begins his prayers by addressing God in the language of love.

With convincing power and relentless consistency, Robert Farrar Capon identifies God as the prototype Lover and a love affair as singularly the best metaphor by which to understand a person's relationship to God. Capon declares, "The glory and the misery of the love affair is the master image for the understanding of our vocation."[8] He explains, "God just wants *us*. And the calling of the beloved is simply to love. . . . The will of God is . . . his longing that we will take the risk of being nothing but ourselves, desperately in love."[9]

Sallie McFague recognizes that though most all people readily affirm the Bible's truth that God is love, some hesitate to take the next logical step of naming God as Lover. McFague responds to those who question the Lover-beloved relationship between God and humanity with questions of her own: "Why, given its importance to and power in human life, has this model *not* been included centrally in Christianity? As the most intimate of all human relationships, as the one that to the majority of people is the most central and precious, the one giving the most joy (as well as the most pain), does it not contain enormous potential? . . . Could a relationship be of such crucial importance in our existence and be irrelevant in our relationship with God?"[10]

The popular Quaker writer Richard Foster describes his best-selling volume on prayer as a book "about a love relationship: an enduring, continuing, growing love relationship with the great God of the universe."[11] Foster counsels his readers, "To be effective pray-ers, we need to be effective lovers."[12]

The love metaphor—God as Lover, a relationship with God as a love affair, and prayer as communion between lovers—dominates the pages which follow. In fact, the new meaning, freedom, and intimacy which I have found in prayer spring from the ministry of this metaphor in my life. My prayers to God stem from a realization of God's love for me and take form as an expression of my love for God. The understanding and practice of prayer center upon and invite you into a love affair with God.

≥∎

Profoundest satisfaction in speaking is not in hearing one's own words; it is in discovering what indescribably wondrous meaning these words can have for one's [lover].

Prentiss L. Pemberton, *Dialogue in Romantic Love*

MEANINGFUL PRAYER

Prayer is conversation with a lover, conversation with the Ultimate Lover actually. Prayer is the language of love. Prayer is an ongoing dialogue between two parties totally in love with each other.

When I began to understand prayer in this manner, I rediscovered prayer as one of the most beneficial and liberating experiences of life. Viewing prayer as the communion which transpires within a love affair dramatically contributes to my awareness of how to pray.

Misperceptions of Prayer

Failure to understand prayer in this manner often leads to misperceptions or misplaced priorities. Most common are:

Mechanical Prayer

Some folks view prayer mechanically. They make effective praying depend upon following a carefully prescribed set of procedures. They approach God in prayer in much the same manner as they begin to put together the parts in a make-your-own-bicycle kit. They follow step-by step directions!

When viewed mechanically, praying to God means meeting certain requirements. It might be a matter of finding the right place and choosing the proper time to pray. It might mean assuming one particular physical posture and adopting a specific mental attitude. Some persons feel they must proceed to pray according to a predetermined sequence which moves, point by point, from adoration of God to intercessions for other people and that their prayer requires that an appropriate amount of time be devoted to each part of the prayer. Stated or implied, the claim is, "Follow these directions and your prayers will be effective."

Magical Prayer

Another common perspective on prayer dangerously flirts with magic. Advocates of this point of view guarantee that certain words and actions get a good response from God. Therefore, prayer requires that meticulous attention be devoted to choosing one term over another and forming phrases in a precise manner.

Tragically, this misunderstanding of prayer tends to reduce important phrases like "in Jesus' name" and "through Jesus Christ our Lord" to the status of an abra-cadabra-type formula which is guaranteed to "work." When their prayers don't "work," frustrated individuals often complain, "I used all the right words, but nothing happened."

Meaningful prayer is neither magical nor mechanical. It is personal and spiritual. Meaningful prayer is the honest talk which occurs between two lovers.

Questions about Prayer

Understanding prayer as communion within a love affair radically alters answers given to the questions which dominate most discussions about prayer. In fact, such an understanding of prayer renders these questions virtually irrelevant.

"How Do You Define Prayer?"

I don't. Neither does the Bible. The Scriptures commend, command, invite, and describe prayer. But the Bible does not define prayer.

Traditionally, religious leaders speak of prayer as communication with God. *Communion* may actually be a better term. Communication implies an exchange of words and logic. Often a prayer consists of nonverbal outcries which are far more emotional than rational. The substance of prayer is communion with God—what John Killenger calls "the act of being with God."[1]

Prayer starts and ends with God the Lover. We pray because God invited (and commanded) us to pray and then made it possible for us to meet this divine expectation. Thus, prayer is a gift—a gift from the loving God which, when properly received by the beloved, becomes that person's reciprocal gift of love to God. In this sense, prayer is the language of a love affair.

"How Should I Address God?"

In the Bible, God is addressed in a variety of ways.[2] No one title for God is superior or "right." However, the words with which people address God ought always convey a reverence born of love.

Jesus most frequently spoke of God as father, sometimes joining the word for father in one language with the same word in another language—"Abba, Father."[3] A redundancy of intimacy! In every instance, Jesus addressed

God with terms indicative of tenderness, compassion, and closeness. For Jesus, God was the essence of love.

How would you speak to One who loves you beyond measure? That is how God should be addressed. Personally, though I see God primarily as "Lover," I find that variety in how I address God helps me avoid falling into a thoughtless routine.

Sometimes I begin a prayer with "Our Father." But I also acknowledge God in other ways: "God of Creation and Redemption"; "God of Life and Death"; "God of Abraham, Isaac, and Jacob"; "God of Sarah, Rachel, and Ruth"; "Great and Good God"; "God of Revelation and Inspiration"; "God of Faith and Hope"; and "Loving God."

To be totally honest, I must confess that sometimes I rush into prayer so hurriedly that I fail to employ any formal mode of address for God. You can do that with your lover, you know. When we urgently need to speak to God, all we have to do is begin speaking—no prelude, no words of address, no hesitations. God is already listening.

"Must Every Prayer Conclude with the Same Words?"

No. No one phrase is sacred (or magical). No one conclusion to prayer has been divinely established. A study of the prayers which appear in the New Testament reveals a wide variety of endings to people's communiqués to God.

"What Kind of Language Should I Use?"

The language which one lover would exchange with another is the language of prayer. No need exists to be more specific than that because no one can tell someone else how to articulate their love.

Prayer is a personal experience of intimacy with God. No two people have to pray alike.

"What Is the Proper Physical Posture for Prayer?"

Another mechanical question. The meaning of prayer is not determined by proper mechanics, but by personal authenticity.

Many people prefer a position conducive to meditation when praying. They may recline in a chair or sit on the floor. Throughout history, the greatest intensity in prayer has been associated with a person lying completely prone on the floor while praying.

The most important consideration is that a person be herself or himself. The "proper position" is the one which most contributes to concentration on communing with God. At times, expressions to a lover erupt so naturally and spontaneously that no thought is given to the place or posture of prayer.

"How Long Should I Pray?"

How long should lovers talk to each other? Neither brevity nor great length is a virtue. Most crucial is an individual taking whatever amount of time she needs to unload her heart before God and to hear God's response.

"Does Prayer Really Work?"

Ah, at last. Often this question comes first.

Actually, it is a bad question. Prayer is not a utilitarian practice aimed at achieving an accomplishment. Neither is prayer an exercise in which a person gets exactly what he asks for if he takes great care to state the request properly.

Prayer is communion with God. Prayer consists of intimate conversations between two lovers. The value of prayer is prayer! To ask if prayer works is to misunderstand the nature of the experience. It's like asking, "Does love work?" or "What do you get out of talking to the one you love?"

Prayer as Loving Communion

In our conversations with God, we need not be preoccupied with the logistics, language, and organization of our concerns. We need only speak to God with absolute candor and a total lack of inhibition. Prayer is an invitation to speak to the One who loves us beyond measure about anything and everything in our lives in any way and in every way without the least fear of God's rejection of us or a diminishment in God's compassion for us.

I wish I had understood prayer in this manner—prayer as talk between two lovers—several years ago when that nameless stranger telephoned me long distance and asked how he should say his prayers. I would have been better off, and so would he. I would have told him to forget how anyone else prays, to focus on the God who loves him with a matchless love, and then to pour out his heart to God. But, at that time, I did not adequately understand either love or prayer.

Things have changed. I thank God as well as all the people who have enlightened my understanding of love and prayer since that time. Amid the changes, though, I have not forgotten that man. This book is for him and others like him who even now journey in quest of an adequate understanding of prayer and a meaningful practice of prayer.

Prayer is a totally free expression of love. Prayer is an act in which we speak with absolute honesty to God, the One who loves us infinitely, the One who is not about to stop loving us. When we pray, we can say anything and everything to God. We can address God regarding all our desires—the good ones and the bad ones and the ones we are trying to decide about. We need not spend time worrying about mechanics or logistics. We need only to focus all our efforts on reaching out to God in complete freedom and honesty. Then, we can experience the relief (and often the exhilaration) of communing with the Lover to whom we can share our innermost thoughts—knowing that whatever we divulge to God will not nullify our acceptance, prevent our opportunity to know forgiveness, or deny us love.

To pray is to talk with God. To pray is to engage in an intimate conversation with the Ultimate Lover. The kind of communion which takes place between two people passionately in love with each other is the kind of dialogue which forms the substance of prayer. Prayer is a response to love as well as an expression of love.

If you know how to communicate with your lover, you know how to speak with God. If you do not know how to carry on dialogue within a loving relationship, perhaps this book will help you. Part 2 elaborates the nature of a loving relationship with God. Part 3 describes the manner in which people in love with God speak to God.

Prayer consists of the language of a love affair. Prayer is communion between two lovers. Praying is one dimension of being in love—being in love with God.

&

PART TWO

*Real prayer comes not from gritting our teeth
but from falling in love.*
Richard Foster, *Finding the Heart's True Home*

Falling in Love with God

The root of the problem of prayer lies in the difficulty of conceiving of God as a personal being.

Georgia Harkness, "The Theology of Prayer"

IMAGING GOD

Love at first sight is rare. It happens, but not often—even in relation to God. Some people would say *especially* in relation to God. Falling in love with God usually takes a good bit of time.

I hate to admit it, but for years I never thought much about loving God. It took a long time for me to fall in love with God because of how I viewed God. The God I saw encouraged fear, reverence, honor, obedience, worship, and various forms of service. But not love. Not until I began to see God as Lover—my Lover, the world's Lover—did I begin to love God, really love God. I wish it had happened earlier, but it didn't. I had been a Christian for many years before I came to understand that God is in love with me, that God desires my love in return, and that I can love God.

With the realization that I *could* (not just *should*) love God came major changes in my relationship to God. Activities I previously saw as duties to be carried out with lip-biting discipline suddenly looked like opportunities for life-enhancing pleasure. A sense of faith as bondage gave way to an appreciation for faith as a life of freedom.

No aspect of my relationship with God was more dramatically altered by this change in perspective than my practice of personal, private prayer. I stopped seeing prayer as a heavy responsibility to be done dutifully and began approaching prayer as an occasion for loving conversation. Logistics and mechanics took a back seat in importance. I realized I could speak to God when alone or in a crowd, silently or audibly, with my eyes wide open staring at a traffic signal or with my eyes closed in intense concentration. I came to understand that all God wants from me is an honest expression of my love at the moment I pray (every time I pray), whether that expression involves praise, confession, a plea, a complaint, intercession, or all of these combined.

How we see God, to a large extent, conditions how we pray to God and how we relate to God.

Inadequate Images of God

Though God never sat for a portrait, certain images of God get passed from generation to generation like the yellowed photographs in a photo album. Some of these images nurture greater devotion and invite more profound communion. Sadly, however, most of them do not. Many of the sober, passed-along images of God discourage, even hurt, personal communion with God.

Divine Abstraction

Most efforts to describe the greatness of God—divine omnipotence, omniscience, and omnipresence—dissolve into meaningless abstractions. Philosophers and moralists seem particularly prone to attempt reducing the unfathomable nature of God to an impressive phrase.

Well-meaning people have proposed that God be seen as "the Prime Mover," "Sovereign of the Universe," "the First Cause," and "the Ground of Being." Others have identified God as "the *Summum Bonum*," "Holy Perfection," and "the Ultimate Bundle of Highest Values."[1]

Such phrases may contribute to a deeper appreciation of divine transcendence, more respect for God's righteousness, and an expanded concept of God's greatness. However, these abstract generalizations depersonalize God and contribute to vagueness in people's thoughts about God. How do we engage in intimate prayer with "the Prime Mover"? Who would ever want to confess a hurtful sin to "Holy Perfection"?

Human Projection

The Bible affirms that every individual is created in the image of God. However, this does not mean that God is like a really great person, but more so. Though a declaration that God is greater than any person is unquestionably true, that assertion leaves far too much unsaid. God is other than any person. To know the very best member of humanity remains light-years away from knowing God. Nevertheless, many people focus their sights on an image of God which looks very much like a giant-sized projection of a familiar person.

Scorekeeper. One of the more popular images of God is that of "Sacred Scorekeeper." People project into the heavenly realm a certified moral accountant who sits at a celestial desk tallying good and bad acts of behavior for every person. The divine bookkeeper constantly updates a monumental spreadsheet so as to know at any moment whether a specific individual is ahead or behind in his or her efforts to please God. Negative numbers spell trouble.

Angry Judge. Closely related to the "scorekeeper" image of God is the concept of God as an "Angry Judge." All of humanity gathers to watch God seated against the backdrop of a heavenly courtroom. Everybody shudders as God propounds the law in a booming voice, waves a heavy gavel in the air, and loudly condemns those who have broken the law—which means all of us. Each person, knowing full well the verdict, waits to hear the sentencing and the punishment.

Heavenly Barterer. Some people see God as the "Heavenly Barterer." God bestows blessings, kindness, and mercy on people who deserve goodness. People who please God assure themselves of God's favor. God owes it to them.

God is a fair dealer. Everybody gets exactly what he or she deserves. People who want to live in God's favor just have to be sure that they say and do all the right things. When life is going poorly, it is a good bet that an individual needs to do better by God.

Political Sovereign. Through the ages, innumerable people have perceived God as a "Political Sovereign." God runs a just kingdom in which bad people are punished and good people are rewarded. Individuals who keep the law, pay taxes and tithes, make offerings, and support right causes succeed. Those who fail have no hope.

Perfect Saint. Often people who have grown up within a church view God as "the Model Ecclesiastical Saint." God is everything a member of a church should be. Disturbed by their own failures in the life of a church, some people may project onto God all they wish they had been or could be.

An image of an ecclesiastical God hurts other people as well as those who hold it. In his wonderful book, *Your God Is Too Small*, J. B. Phillips describes the danger. "If the churches give the outsider the impression that God works almost exclusively through the machinery they have erected and . . . damns all other machinery which does not bear their label, then they cannot be surprised if he finds their version of God cramped and inadequate and refuses to 'join their union.'"[2]

Each of these descriptions of God has just enough truth in it to prevent a quick and outright dismissal of it, but not enough truth in it to serve as a valid picture of the Almighty. All the descriptions contain concepts of power, goodness, sovereignty, anger, and judgment from a human perspective. None makes an allowance for the mercy, grace, and forgiveness that are unique to God.

What's more, the best of human projections about the nature of God fail to encourage intimate communion with God. Why would a person ever speak to God confessionally when trying to win the favor of the divine scorekeeper or avoid the wrath of an angry judge? Would a person not choose to be silent before God rather than run the risk of sharing concerns which could prompt God to respond negatively?

Personal Reactions

All of these pictures of God spark personal reactions. But, what kind?

Certainly, God commands awe, respect, and reverence. To stand (or kneel) in the presence of the Being who was before time, the Power who started creation moving, the Epitome of all that is right and good, would be overwhelming. No doubt, awe would border on fear and reverence on a desire to run.

To be sure, God deserves awe, respect, and reverence from us. However, according to the Bible, God desires for each of these emotions to contribute to closeness, not distance—communion, not separation or isolation.

At times we may fear God. Typically, our fear consists more of anxiety over the unknown—what will the future hold?—than of a dread of danger. Fear can be the beginning of understanding. However, fear held too long becomes a serious problem. The better we get to know God, the less likely we are to fear God. In the Bible, every time a revelation from God prompted fear among people, God acted quickly to declare, "Fear not" (e.g. Isa. 41:10; 43:1).

Love is compatible with awe, respect, and reverence. At its best, love causes a lover to look upon the beloved with all these emotions. Not with fear, though. Where love prevails, fear disappears.

Unfortunately, many of the more popular human projections of God incite fear rather than nurture love. The result is people so fearful of God that it never occurs to them to love God. Distorted images of God provoked terror within Martin Luther, driving him "to the very abyss of despair." Luther exclaimed, "I wished I had never been created. Love God? I hated him!"[3] I understand. Though my fear of God never turned into hatred, it successfully kept me from loving God.

A religion of fear has neither the time nor the inclination for love. Involvement in worship stems from a fear of not worshiping rather than from a God-oriented heart filled with love and wonder. A commitment to Jesus Christ forms as a means of avoiding God's wrath and escaping hell rather than as an expression of love which opens the way into abundant life and a pilgrimage in which service is a source of joy. Doing good becomes a way of escaping the punishment designed for those who do wrong rather than serving as the declaration of a love for God which finds delight in morally responsible behavior.

Prayer suffers and dies in fear-based religion. Hounded by fright, an individual cannot pour out his heart to God in adoration, praise, thanksgiving, intercession, confession, repentance, or commitment. The person cannot really concentrate on what he needs to share with God for fear that he is not using the right words, assuming the proper posture, following a prescribed formula, or otherwise expressing himself in a manner acceptable to the easily angered God.

Where fear reigns, faith shrinks. And dread denies love a chance to be born. Meaningful prayer is out of the question. Good news demands attention, though. God is love—perfect love, the Perfect Lover. Love invites, indeed longs for, conversation. Conversation contributes to communion. God welcomes communion with us regardless of our life situations. And, as the Bible declares, perfect love casts out fear.

God as Lover

A young man, recently ordained, dressed carefully. He felt good about himself and wanted his appearance to project a pastoral happiness to others. As he walked the streets of his city, the young fellow wandered into a bad neighborhood. Already uncomfortable, he realized that a drunk man was watching him closely, obviously unimpressed by what he saw. Suddenly, the eyes of the two men met. When that happened, the inebriated man spoke, "Sonny, what do you know about God?" The newly ordained minister could not respond. He quickly returned to his room, took off his clerical garb, and sat pondering the question, "What do I know about God?"[4]

What a great question! For everybody. It's a question well worth pondering—and answering. Given the inadequate images of God which hinder meaningful communion, let us take an inventory of what we know about God.

Jesus Christ provides us with the best insights into who God is. Though we can never fully comprehend the nature of God—"God defined is God finished," a Frenchman observed—when we look at Jesus we see what God is like. Every facet of Jesus' life and ministry brings clarity about some aspect of the God of love—God the Lover.

Incarnation—"God with Us"

Though the language is philosophical, the truth it announces is both emotional and personal: "And the Word became flesh and lived among us" (John 1:14). At a specific moment in history, in the life of a particular person named Jesus, God took up residence among people on earth. One of the names assigned to the Christ child carries in it the fundamental purpose of the Bethlehem nativity and the essential meaning of the incarnation—Emmanuel, which means "God with us" (Isa. 7:14; Matt. 1:23).

God's love for people had been established long ago. But few, if any folks could conceive of the full meaning of this love. When God took on flesh, accepted the humiliation of being at the mercy of the human race, and used the humanity of Jesus to invite people into greater intimacy, the nature of God's love began to be understood as never before. And what a love it is.

In the incarnation, God erased all boundaries between the sacred and the secular, the mundane and the spectacular, the holy and the ordinary. The arrival of Emmanuel signaled God's presence in the world and availability to all people in all times and circumstances. God's love will not abandon anyone. The God who slipped into this world via a manger in the little one-camel town of Bethlehem is the God who will join people in the most difficult places and the harshest moments of their lives, as well as in the best of times.

If ever we find ourselves about to abandon hope, to argue for a closed universe, to confess disappointment that we have been forgotten, or to assert that no one loves us, the truth of the incarnation contradicts our conclusions. The reality of Emmanuel stirs our souls and breaks into our darkness. We can believe again, hope again, have faith again, and love again. God is with us. And beyond any shadow of a doubt, God loves us.

Ministry and Message—"Good News"

If any question about God's love for the world and all people in it remained immediately after the birth of Jesus, surely the life and ministry of Jesus answered that question. Through sermons, lessons, parables, healings, caring, and works of mercy, Jesus identified God as a lover—really, *The* Lover.

Jesus revealed a God whose love knows no bounds or conditions and whose expectations of us center on love. In a story about the great judgment, Jesus spoke of God bestowing eternal life only upon persons who had lived by love not just talked about love (Matt. 25:31–46). By way of a parable about two young men who nearly broke their father's heart (Luke 15:11–32), Jesus discussed how God's love sets aside tendencies toward paybacks and revenge in order to extend a welcome, an embrace, forgiveness, restoration, and celebration to a penitent traitor.

Through both actions and words, Jesus established the truth that God is not an enemy to be avoided, a tyrant to be appeased. All who look at the ministry of Jesus and study God's message learn that all of God's activity is loving. God creates in love, sustains in love, and judges in love. God's anger is an expression of that love; God's redemption is an act of love.

The New Testament letters which bear the name of John provide a wonderful commentary on the ministry and message of Jesus. This writer powerfully underscored the reality of God's love revealed in Jesus: "God's love was revealed among us in this way: God sent his only Son into the world so that we might live through him. In this is love, not that we loved God but that he loved us and sent his Son to be the atoning sacrifice for our sins" (1 John 4:9–10).

Crucifixion—Suffering Love

Nowhere is the nature of God more fully revealed in the experience of Jesus than at the crucifixion. One writer commented, "The crucified Jesus is the only accurate picture of God the world has ever seen."[5]

New Testament writers understood the crucifixion of Jesus as a revelation of God's love. Paul captured the staggering truth most succinctly, "God proves his love for us in that while we still were sinners Christ died for us" (Rom. 5:8). Not even misunderstanding, anger, and outright rejection could discourage or deter God's love. At the worst moment possible, God offered the greatest gift of love imaginable.

In the crucifixion of Jesus, God embraced the whole of humanity. No one was left out. "For God so loved the world" is the way John said it (John 3:16). The ancient Cyril of Jerusalem put the truth another way, "On the cross God stretched out his hands to embrace the ends of the earth."[6]

The idea of a suffering God, a thought which some people find repulsive, can be found only in Christianity. But suffering love stands at the heart of the gospel. Jesus reveals the God who loves people so much that no individual is left to bear any loneliness, cruelty, or rejection that God has not known. No person ever has to endure any dimension of life, not even suffering, alone. God takes our suffering into the Divine Being.

What amazing love! The omnipotent God willfully accepted suffering in order to create the possibility of redemption for all people, even for those people who killed God's Son. In a mindboggling act of love, God took the evil-inspired murder of the innocent Messiah and graciously transformed that event into an opportunity for new life. What a Lover![7]

The crucifixion of Jesus is an unmitigated act of revelation from God. Behind the cross of Jesus stands God the Lover. The cross itself serves as an exclamation point regarding the priority of love in the nature and will of God. From the cross comes a reminder of the necessity of suffering within a redemptive life guided by God's kind of love. Reflection on the cross produces a realization of the unbreakable union between suffering and love.

Resurrection—Triumphant Love

What appeared to be the end of Jesus was not the end at all. It was only a new beginning. Even after the crucifixion of Jesus, God was not through speaking about love and demonstrating the nature of love through Jesus. God's last act of love in Jesus' life on earth left no person (none of us) untouched by the possibilities of love. God raised Jesus from the dead!

God chose to accomplish redemption by working through creation. In the midst of human history—"in the fullness of time"—God became a person—"you shall call his name Jesus." And God refused to allow the life of Jesus to be snuffed out. The resurrection of Jesus dramatically heralds God's love for creation and reveals love's relentless press toward redemption.

The resurrection of Jesus conveys God's love for humanity and demonstrates what every person can (and should) be. We do not have to deny our human nature or seek to escape it in order to please God. To recognize the truth of the resurrection of Jesus is to receive an invitation from God—a summons not only to be human but to be fully human. God loves human beings.

The resurrection of Jesus also demonstrates the power of God's stubborn grace, perhaps the most characteristic aspect of God's love. People—people like us—had made their wishes known and taken action to have their way. Jesus was dead. Killed! But God would have the last word. Instead of retaliation or condemnation, God responded with resurrection. What opponents of Jesus intended as death, God transformed into a means of new life. Scowls and insults from people pleased to see Jesus dead were met head-on by promises of peace and invitations to faith by the God who brought Jesus from the tomb.

What unfathomable love! Every aspect of Jesus' life verifies the legitimacy of viewing God as Lover—none, though, more than the resurrection.

Conclusions

Now, back to the question of "What do we know about God?" Standing in the light radiating from the life and ministry of Jesus, we can see certain traits of God's nature very clearly and come to a few fundamental conclusions about God.

God is love. If that truth was hinted, suspected, and whispered in the Old Testament, it was shouted in the revelation of God through Jesus. No insight into God's nature is more self-evident in the life of Jesus than this—God is love.

But God is much more than love. Love *is* the essence of God's being. However, to elevate love to the status of a deity is to practice idolatry. Love is not God; God is love.

God loves us. Every one of us! The strength and longing of God's love for us revealed in the teachings of Jesus sometimes overwhelm us. Take, for example, Jesus' parable of the waiting, loving father. Consider the old man standing in the middle of a dusty road squinting his eyes as he peers into the distance trying to catch a glimpse of his wayward son returning home. That father looks like God. And the pilgrim son could be any one of us—male or female. See the old patriarch as he finally spots a speck on the distant horizon, watches it until he can make out the profile of his son, and then casts dignity aside, sprinting to embrace the child who had turned his back on him. The father in the parable embodies the kind of surging passion which found expression in the Bible's extended hymn of love called the Song of Songs. Here is a powerful, unforgettable picture of God as Lover.

Meister Eckhart boldly stated the truth about God usually discovered by all who come to know God intimately. "God is foolishly in love with us. It seems he has forgotten heaven and earth and all his happiness and deity; entire business seems with me alone."[8] Of course, the love is not for one person to the exclusion of others. It's for everybody.

Coming to understand God as Lover creates a new outlook into the meaning and nature of prayer. In the context of God's love, prayer no longer looks like a religious duty which we must perform to be religiously secure. Prayer is a wonderful opportunity to engage and interact with God the Lover, to enjoy a soul-lightening form of communion in which honesty and vulnerability nurture greater intimacy, to experience a vast array of redemptive gifts, and to learn the wisdom which makes possible a life of love.

❧

CHAPTER FOUR

Ah, blessed Lord, I wish I knew how I might best love you . . .
that my love were as sweet to you as your love is to me.

Margery Kempe

DEFINING LOVE

Love is a slippery word. People mean radically different things when they claim to "love" ice cream, a certain make of car, a husband or a wife, a piece of music, or God. But you cannot prove it by their vocabulary. In fact, most people probably declare their love for chocolate pie more often than they claim to love God.

You don't have to be an anthropologist or a sociologist to realize that culture powerfully shapes how we understand love. Simply listen to popular music, go to movies, look at advertisements, and read best-sellers.

Our society adores love. We plead for love, laugh about love, cry over love, celebrate love, and grieve because of love. Storytellers guarantee themselves large audiences by weaving one tale after another about love affairs. Public relations firms sell everything from automobiles to toothpaste with images of love and promises of love. Love enjoys a highly elevated status in our society. "We symbolize it, study it, worship it, idealize it, applaud it, fear it, envy it, live for it, and die for it."[1] We think about it, sing about it, write about it, preach about it, and brag about it.

But, what is the "it"? What is the nature of the love with which our culture is in love? And, is this kind of love appropriate within our relationship to God?

Many of us believe the Bible offers the best definition of love. When we think of love, we probably think of 1 Corinthians 13, the most exquisite portrait of love in literature, the most complete understanding of love in the Scriptures. However, the Bible also contains other, very different concepts of love.

For example, the most common Old Testament term for love, *ahebh*, refers to the intimate, passionate relationship formed by personal love between a man and a woman. As the prophets, who were the first to describe God's relationship to people in terms of love, began to define the love of God, they elevated the meaning of *ahebh*, replacing the impulsive nature of love between persons with love marked by a "deliberate direction of the will and readiness for action."[2]

The great commandment to love God (Deut. 6:5) assumes a similar kind of love—a love which willfully focuses on God and works to sustain obedience and fidelity to God. People are mandated to love God with loyalty and integrity akin to that in God's love for them—a love which, rather than ceasing in the face of betrayal, reaches out to the betrayer with an offer of forgiveness and restoration. What is more, God makes possible in people the quality of love God expects from people. We learn how to love God by living in the love with which God has loved us.

Which of these loves dwells in us? Is our concept of love influenced more by culture or by Scripture? What about our practice of love? When we speak of loving God or being in love with God, what do we mean?

Honestly, for most of us, answering those questions is a mixed bag. Our understanding of love has been shaped by both biblical texts and social relationships. The fabric of our love for God is woven with yarn spun from all the various kinds of love.

Kinds of Love

Separating different kinds of love from each other and drawing hard and fast lines between them are almost impossible tasks. In the Bible, as in contemporary culture, almost every loving relationship involves more than one type of love—each with different shades of meaning, each intermingling with and influencing the others. Most expressions of love defy neat categories. For purposes of discussion and better understanding, however, I will attempt to distinguish between three distinctly different kinds of love. Each of these types of love appears both in the Bible and in contemporary society.

Eros: **Romantic Love**

More than four hundred years prior to the birth of Jesus, philosophers like Plato wrote extensively about erotic love.[3] Since that time, perceptive people have recognized the presence of eros in the lives of lovers. Major disagreements have arisen, however, over whether eros is a positive or negative factor in loving relationships.

Many people consider eros a negative force, an evil passion, a drive singularly focused on self-fulfillment. Physical features in one person strike fires of passion in another person. As a result, the individual desperately wants the other, desiring closeness to, if not union with, the other person.

However, erotic passion focuses not so much on communion with the individual desired as on the fulfillment of desire. Critics of eros often argue that the object of desire in erotic love is almost inconsequential as long as the desire itself is satisfied.[4]

Romance. Much of the criticism directed at eros generally stems from negative reactions to one particular type of erotic love known as romantic love. But, romantic love belongs in a special category. The word *romance* derives from an old French word, *roman*, meaning a novel or a story written in the style of a district in southern France called Provence. Across the years, this term has come to denote the courtly love popularized by ancient troubadours.

Beauty sparks romantic love—the attracting, captivating beauty of the beloved. Then, romantic attraction to that beautiful person afflicts a would-be lover with restlessness, fainting, sleeplessness, and deep sighing. Passion courses through the lover motivating and energizing his commitment to chivalrous actions. Ironically, the lover may come to enjoy the suffering of romance almost as much as contact with his beloved.

Classic romantic love is a game. A suitor sets out to win the favor of a beautiful woman. Barriers to love and imposing possibilities of failure make the chase more fun. The lover vows to his beloved that he will go anywhere and do anything to win her affection.

A true romantic wants only a glance, a smile, or a nod of approval from his beloved, not physical union or a long-term relationship—certainly not marriage. Having once won attention from the object of his affection, the man well may be off in pursuit of the attention of another beauty. That's how the romantic game is played.[5]

The language of romance is all about us. People admire the "blind passion" of young lovers and praise couples who seem to be "insanely in love." A preoccupied public seems almost dazed by the romantic talk which goes on between lovers: "You are all I want; nothing else in life matters." "Your wish is my command. I want to spend my life pleasing you." "I know you cannot provide for me economically, but you are spontaneous, chivalrous, heroic, and self-sacrificing. What more could anyone ask for in life?"

Romance is not all bad, not by any means. Romantic love can enhance life and contribute to the durable quality of loving relationships.[6] But, it's not automatic, and it's not a game.

Used wrongly, romance can become little more than a strategy for getting what one wants—a tool of manipulation. Romantic interests tend to gravitate toward receiving love rather than giving love. Without the balance and influence of other affections, romance can even become an addiction or an obsession. When that happens, "Love becomes a drug, and the loved one becomes the addicted lover's 'fix.'"[7]

Abuses and extreme examples of romantic love cause us to raise questions about its validity within relationships. But distortions of romantic love should not blind us to the real thing. From a Christian point of view, romantic love claims its rightful place in any truly loving relationship. Far more than a preoccupation with artful romantic "lines" and a mastery of etiquette, romance is "a quality of deepening affection . . . in which the distinctive feature is an experience of total communication between those who love."[8] Each lover seeks to overcome self-centeredness and selfishness in the relationship by practicing forgiveness, trust, and reconciliation. Neither lover is in love with love; each is in love with the other.

Beauty remains an important factor in romance. However, the beauty of each lover does not create love between them so much as the love between them causes each to see the other as beautiful.

Personal and Relational Value. Unbridled, selfish desire does not represent a true portrait of eros. Neither do bizarre episodes of romantic love tell the whole story of erotic love.

More and more people are coming to recognize the personal and relational value of erotic love. Joanne Stroud asserts, "As passion—Eros introduces changes, disturbances, feelings that move us into connection," that move the soul to a new awareness.[9] Indeed, eros is often associated with affection, a word unburdened by negative connotations. C. S. Lewis rejected the idea that a lover motivated by eros only uses the person desired to fulfill selfish needs. He wrote, "In some mysterious but quite indisputable fashion the lover desires the Beloved herself, not the pleasure she can give."[10]

When eros matures as a form of love, even its tendency toward selfishness dramatically diminishes. Lovers influenced by erotic love would rather be together in unhappiness than separated from each other in happiness. Each values the presence of the other more than pleasure. Frankly, this sounds a lot like an important dimension of Christian discipleship. I would rather be in a difficult situation with Jesus than on easy street without Him.

The greatest temptation of eros may reside within its beauty and power. Indeed, historically, theologians have feared erotic love because of its propensity for idolatry. Lovers may become more committed to eros than to each other, more excited about falling in love than interested in being in love. As a servant of lovers, erotic love enhances a relationship. If elevated to the status of a deity, however, erotic love quickly becomes demonic.

To be sure, erotic love is not the most mature form of love, not the highest quality of love, not the closest in kin to divine love. Yet, when brought under the influence of the gospel and thus expressed with fidelity, self-sacrifice, reverence, and grace, erotic love can contribute immeasurably to the health, stability, and enjoyment of a loving relationship.

But, what, if anything, does eros have to do with our love for God? Several theologians consistently and loudly have answered this question with, "Nothing!" They argue that eros has no place at all in a person's love for God. Anders Nygren went so far as to say that a person cannot love God in any way. According to Nygren, people only can have faith in God; individuals are incapable of loving God.[11]

God, as revealed in the Bible, desires the love of humanity. In fact, God has commanded such love. Why would God not welcome a person's warm affection as well as that individual's reasoned obedience? God wills to be served by all that we are and have. "Christian love . . . cannot be perfected without the warmth of personal affection."[12] "Eros enraptures the soul in committed engagement."[13]

Forget the negative stereotypes which usually accompany a mention of eros. Set aside the tendency to understand eros exclusively in terms of sexuality. And consider erotic love as "a constant desiring, a forever reaching out, a quest for communion with another."[14] Then the legitimacy of eros in a person's love for God becomes clear. As one commentator proposes, "A love for God devoid of passion and power does little to gladden either the human or the divine heart."[15]

Neither the imagery nor the language of erotic love is foreign to the Scriptures studied by Christians or to the spirituality practiced by Christians. From the third century to the nineteenth century, church leaders understood the Old Testament book Song of Songs, a celebration of sensuous love between man and woman, as "an allegory of the prayerful [note: prayerful] communion of the religious person and God."[16] Frequently, persons who had dedicated their lives to loving God and praying to God spoke to God through the vocabulary of romantic love.

In the Old Testament, desire births love and serves as an impetus to enlightenment. Louise Cowan believes "The Psalms, the Song of Songs, Isaiah, and Lamentations quite overtly present the lyric eros in their yearning for the fullness of Yahweh's presence."[17] Certainly some sections of the Psalms ring with a passion for God which sounds like eros. Psalm 42 is representative.

> *As a deer longs*
> *for flowing streams,*
> *so my soul longs*
> *for you, O God.*
> *My soul thirsts for God,*
> *for the living God.*
> *When shall I come and behold*
> *the face of God?*
>
> Psalm 42:1–2

The word *eros* does not appear in the New Testament. Neither can we find in the Gospels and Epistles sensuous expressions of love similar to those of Psalm 42 (and Ps. 63). However, shortly after the New Testament era, expressions of erotic love became standard fare in many people's prayers to God.

Numerous individuals in the early church addressed God by means of the language and imagery of love. Augustine, who understood prayer as nothing but love, prayerfully confessed to God, "Our heart is restless until it finds its rest in thee."[18] The unknown author of an early book called "Acts of Peter" prayed to God, "O love unspeakable and inseparable."[19] Perceiving God as "our clothing, who wraps and enfolds us for love, embraces us and shelters us, surrounds us for his love, which is so tender that he may never desert us," Julian of Norwich addressed the Trinity as "our everlasting lover."[20]

Admittedly, the manner in which these ancient believers addressed God strikes us as strange. Thomas à Kempis wrote, "My God, my Love, Thou art all mine, and I am all Thine."[21] Similarly, Gertrude More declared to God, "O Love, Love, even by naming thee, my soul loseth itself in thee."[22] Today, even very devout Christians hesitate to apply the terminology of lovers to God. Remember, though, in the lives of our distant predecessors in the faith, the vocabulary of erotic love conjured up no risque images, no thoughts of illicit sexual behavior, and no consciousness of a relationship built upon physical satisfaction. The passionate terminology with which these devoted people of long ago spoke to God represented love in its deepest and fullest sense, a love eager to commit all of life to God.[23]

Conscientiously nurturing a love for God—the God who can never be possessed—leads to spiritual growth and a maturing of God-directed love. Learning how to commune with God without seeking to grasp or control God (natural tendencies) refines our passion. The ultimate result of such spiritual practice is a transformation by which passion becomes devotion and a discovery of how the fullness of love can be experienced in one's own heart.[24]

From the perspective of Christianity, eros is a valid expression of love. Erotic passions have a place within a love affair—even in a love affair with God. However, in a relationship with God, eros is best understood and most responsibly expressed in interaction with other types of love.

Philia: The Love of a Friend

Ancient thinkers prized friendship as the ultimate form of human love.[25] In early Greek culture, the verb which meant to befriend someone (*phileo*) conveyed images of strong feelings, even intense passion. People considered the reciprocity of married love to be a perfect model of friendship.

Friendships form when people share mutual interests, dreams, goals, and problems. No sense of duty dominates friendship. True friends do not "have" each other or "possess" each other quite so much as they "literally let each other be."[26] Friendship is a strong expression of love.

The Greek word *phileo*, properly translated "to love" appears twenty-five times in the New Testament. Originally, philia (the noun) designated a strong feeling for another person—a sentiment associated with liking. Another Greek word, *agape* (from the verb agapao), denoted the stronger emotion of love. However, these two words cannot be sharply distinguished from one another. Several New Testament writers use philia and agape synonymously.[27]

In a very fine book on friendship, Martin Marty measures the nature of friendship by four essential characteristics of love.[28] First, love rejoices over the existence of the beloved. So does friendship. Friends rejoice over each other, celebrating their relationship as a gift from God. Second, love expresses gratitude for the existence of the beloved and readily accepts all that the beloved gives. Likewise with friendship. As Marty asserts, "The fact that the friend is open to my existence, able to affirm and confirm me, is something for which I have gratitude not to that friend, but to God."[29] Third, love contains an element of reverence which protects each lover's distinctiveness and keeps an appropriate distance between them. The same can be said of friendship. Friends do not try to duplicate each other or absorb one another. Rather, they blend intimacy and individuality. Fourth, love nurtures unselfish loyalty to the beloved. Similarly, friendship embraces sacrifice. Friends readily take on hardships for the benefit of each other. Indeed, Jesus indicated that no greater love exists than that in which a person lays down his life for a friend (John 15:13).

Marty arrives at a widely shared conclusion: friendship and love—philia and agape—are very similar, but not identical. "A friend's relation to a friend is a 'simile of the relation to God.'"[30]

Though the concept of friendship love (philia) was foreign to the Old Testament world, the Old Testament contains one of the most beautiful pictures of this kind of love. Mourning the death of Jonathan, David laments, "I am distressed for you, my brother Jonathan; greatly beloved were you to me; your love to me was wonderful, passing the love of women" (2 Sam. 1:26).

Friendship love appears in the New Testament. Though no writer uses *philia* to describe the love of God or erotic love, passages such as Luke 11:5–8 picture God as the best friend a person can have, a friend who grants friends' requests and delights in being asked. Early Christians read a scripture like Matthew 11:19 as a parable enacting God's love for sinners, a parable bearing the message that God offers friendship to sinners.[31]

Like other forms of love, friendship can deteriorate into a self-serving enterprise. However, when friendship develops because the whole personality of another gives pleasure and that feeling is mutually shared, friendship can foreshadow agape love and greatly enhance erotic love.[32] What a terrific pleasure it is for two persons mightily attracted to each other to discover that, among all the other joys of their relationship, they are friends. C. S. Lewis wrote of friendship, "This love, free from instinct, free from all duties but those which love has freely assumed, almost wholly free from jealousy, and free without qualification from the need to be needed, is eminently spiritual."[33]

Translators of the Today's English Version of the Bible demonstrated the spiritual value of friendship love by equating reconciliation and friendship-making in their translation of 2 Corinthians 5:15–21. "Our message is that God was making all mankind his friends through Christ" (v. 19). God's act of reconciliation through Christ involved changing people "from enemies into his [God's] friends" (v. 18). God commissions Christians to "the task of making others his [God's] friends also" (v. 18).

Friendship between a person and God values the mutual concerns of the well-being of the earth and the redemption of humanity. Within that free relationship between friends, bonding occurs. Love grows. Trust and commitment develop.[34]

The work of friendship looks very much like the loving communion which is prayer. Eugene Kennedy described the work of friendship as a continuous effort to keep a friend in focus, "to keep listening even after you think you have heard everything, to understand when you would prefer to be understood, to choose the relationship knowing that it is not free, that there is a price to pay, a death to be accepted as the condition of richer life."[35] What an excellent description of a person's loving relationship with God! Little wonder the seventeenth-century French preacher Jean Baptiste Massillon understood prayer as speaking with God "as a friend to a friend."[36]

Agape: God's Kind of Love

No other word for love reaches the depth and breadth of meaning which characterize the kind of love represented by the Greek term *agape*—God's kind of love.

Romance, eros, and friendship are often called "natural" forms of love. Each of these types of love grows out of natural interests and desires in people's lives. Love which arises within the human heart is, for the most part, need-based love. Not so with agape. The love which comes from God is sheer gift. By its very nature agape is self-giving love, not self-seeking.

God's kind of love involves both will and action. God chooses to love us. As an act of love, God grants freedom to all people—a freedom which allows us to reject God as well as to accept God, to ignore God as well as to love God. When we distance ourselves from God and live contrary to God's will, God chooses to keep on loving us. Not only that, God acts lovingly. God sends the Messiah to secure the possibility of redemption for the very people who turn their backs on God and reject divine love.

God's love is consistent with every other aspect of the divine nature. God's self-giving love complements God's holiness, righteousness, and mercy—the God who is Holiness, Righteousness, and Mercy. God's love reveals the nature of God's Being. "God is love" (1 John 4:16).

The pinnacle of God's revelation coincides with the ultimate definition of love: the Incarnation of Jesus Christ. One theologian has contended that if a person does not understand God's incarnation in Christ as the essence of the self-giving of God, that person will never understand the meaning of love, agape love that is. "The word 'Love' acquires its new meaning through the fact that in Jesus, the 'Suffering Servant of the Lord,' God comes to us."[37]

In the cross of Christ, as nowhere else, agape distinguishes itself from every other form of love. The redemptive death of the innocent Savior uniquely dramatizes the overwhelming power of self-giving love, God's kind of love. Here is unconditional love, forgiving love, merciful love, love without limits—a love which appears absurd and foolish to people who know love only in terms of their own needs and desires. Any person who wonders about the nature of God's love has only to look at the cross of Christ to see in full the radical dimensions of divine compassion.

New Testament writers ascribe agape to individuals as well as to God. We are to love each other with God's kind of love. But, how is that possible? If agape is God's kind of love, how can a finite, imperfect person hope to express agape, even in relation to God? The answer to that question resides in the heart of God's revelation. God enables us to do what the Bible commands, invites, and requests. God's love makes it possible for us to love God as well as other people with a love which approaches the nature of agape even if sometimes it fails. Not only do we love because God loved us (1 John 4:19), we are enabled to love by means of God's love. The only times our love exists without limits and conditions are when we love "in Christ."[38]

Love for God

When C. S. Lewis set out to write his volume on different kinds of love, he wanted to contend that no form of human love should be called love. Lewis intended to prove that unless the love within an individual closely resembles the Love which is God, that person's emotion should be called something other than love. In the course of his study, however, Lewis discovered that he could not easily draw sharp distinctions between various types of love. Lewis concluded that even need-love, which initially he had considered antithetical to God's kind of love, has a rightful place in a person's approach to God. By the very nature of personhood, every individual must love God with a need-based love, at least at first.[39]

I appreciate Lewis' struggle with the meaning of love, especially love for God. I know firsthand the toll exacted by such a wrestling match with definitions.

A Personal Struggle

After I found such great help in the metaphor of prayer as communion within a love affair, I began to question which, if any, of the various expressions of love between human lovers had any place in my conversations with God. Early on, I was tempted to focus on agape alone—to speak to God only in the language of Scripture, theology, and classic piety. But I had a problem with that approach.

My love for God embraces elements of affection not usually associated with agape. Despite knowing that these feelings are a vital part of who I am and that God wants me to be honest about myself when I pray, for a long time I was hesitant. I had never seen some of the sentiments which I wanted to share with God commonly associated with agape. Though they honestly reflected my feelings about God, I did not know what to do with them. When I attempted to convey my emotions through words, the words didn't sound like the language of conventional prayer.

Aware that dishonesty makes a mockery of prayer, I finally understood that God wants to hear how I feel. It does not matter whether or not my expressions are "traditional" as long as my prayers accurately reflect who I am. The God who loves me wants to hear from me in my own words, words born in the crucible of my personal experience.

All of these words and the sentiments behind them—the good and the not so good—get mixed up together. What they do have in common, though, is an orientation to God which is filled with love. That is enough.

When a person truly loves God, agape exists alongside other forms of love and influences the quality of those loves. Agape complements, influences, purifies, and utilizes the other types of love with which we reach out to God.

Romantic Love

The language of romantic love often contributes to meaningful prayer. How can a person know God and not be attracted to God, not be captivated by God's beauty? But the romance reflects the influence of God's kind of love. Agape prevents romance from becoming a game one plays with God; it prohibits the lover from becoming more interested in love than in God.

True to the best spirit of romance, people who pray seek to please God. We find pleasure in pleasing our Beloved. Romantic passion can prompt the kind of adoration of God and praise for God which God invites and the Scriptures commend. Real affection for God is required if an individual is to hunger and thirst after righteousness and seek God's kingdom above all else.

Eros Love

In a sex-saturated society, most people have trouble separating personal desires from sexual drives. Thus, erotic love gets stereotyped as an exclusively sexual form of love. Obviously, then, people hesitate, if not refuse, to speak of erotic love in relation to God. That is unfortunate.

Eros represents a love which is filled with desire. And desire has a place in a person's love for God. An erotic love for God is a love for God which is full of desire for God. Expressions of human passion ultimately lead the lover into the Passion of God.

Recognizing the acute sensitivity of eros, Thomas Moore observed, "A person can live erotically every minute of the day by valuing deep pleasures, beauty, body, adornment, decoration, texture, and color—all things we too often consider secondary or even frivolous."[40] Such sensitive living appropriately parallels and contributes to honest prayers of detailed praise and thanksgiving.

Eros conditioned by agape provides helpful language by which a person can speak to God. Communion with God takes place because of a person's longing for communion with God, not just for communion.

A paradox arises at this point. Lovers of God seek communion with God because in that communion are pleasure, meaning, and joy. However, communion with God also carries with it a strong possibility of suffering. The pleasure of reaching out to God positions a person to experience pain.

At the very moment we know the joy of complete openness before God in communion, God may lead us to become involved in hurtful situations and to ministries accompanied by discomfort. Unredeemed erotic love runs in the face of this reality. However, eros influenced by agape accepts both the suffering and pleasure which accompany communion with God.

Philia Love

To voice a philia type of love for God represents a move beyond duty. To focus freely on God and reach out to God for communion indicates a genuine attraction to God and an interest in walking through life—both the good times and the bad times—with God.

A combination of agape and philia produces a powerful commitment to God. People who possess this commitment both love God and like God. Besides that, they want to live in unbroken communion with God.

57

Passionate Prayer

Prayers born of passions, attractions, will, affection, desires, and self-giving commitment set before God the weaknesses as well as the strengths of our love. We need not be coy about our faults and failures in love. God already knows us better than we know ourselves. We trust the Lover God to receive our prayers (and us) with understanding, forgiveness, and grace.

That is all we can do; that is all God asks us to do. And we need not worry about it. The God who invites our prayers is the God who loves us immeasurably and always responds to us with merciful love.

To love God and to be loved by God is to experience the freedom to speak honestly with God. Prayer, then, exists as welcome communion within a love affair. The constancy and integrity of such prayer produce an energizing, redeeming intimacy between the lovers.

❧

CHAPTER FIVE

"Is it easy to love God?" asks an old author.
"It is easy," he replies, "to those who do it."

C. S. Lewis, *The Four Loves*

LOVING GOD

Loving God may not be easy, at least not at first. Frankly, some individuals have trouble loving anybody! They resist the demands of love more than they long for the blessings of love. But the deal is that the two go together. Love involves gifts and demands, blessings and responsibilities. Try to get one without the other and the whole deal is off.

God loves us. That reality is the beginning of everything. Along with the gift of God's love comes the responsibility for reciprocal love—we are to love God. Lest we view responsive love as a burden, though, a combination of the Bible, history, and personal experience teaches us that the opportunity—not duty—to love God is one of life's greatest pleasures.

We may not fall in love with God at first sight, especially if our initial imagery of God is faulty. Our love for God may develop slowly rather than quickly, and that is OK. God makes it possible for us to love because of God's gift of love to us. As the Scriptures state, "We love because He [God] first loved us" (1 John 4:19).

Our love for God develops neither as an act of courage nor as an initiative of our creativity, but as an expression of reciprocity. We are invited to participate in a love affair with One who is totally in love with us and in possession of plenty of evidence to prove that love.

As our love for God intensifies, our desire for contact with God grows. Then, the more contact we experience, the more we know about God, and the more profound our love becomes. Our love for God leads to communion with God. And our communion with God strengthens our love for God. The communion which transpires within this love affair is prayer. We find ourselves caught up in praying to God as a result of being in love with God.

A life of prayer is a life of love, and vice versa. Each nurtures the other. Every aspect of being in love with God contributes to meaningful prayer, which embraces every aspect of being in love.

All the dimensions of a love affair, from its inception through its maturation, appear in the life of prayer. Four major aspects of loving God, each of which is an important attribute of genuine personal communion with God, verify that truth.

Appreciating Mystery

Why do two people feel so strongly about one another? What caused their initial attraction? What on earth do they see in each other? How do they find so much pleasure in just being together?

The Mystery of Love

Trying to explain love is like trying to define beauty or to analyze devotion. Love does not yield its secrets in response to careful analysis or surgical dissection. Love cannot be charted on a graph or diagrammed as a sentence. It defies scientific formulas. Love is more than what is known, more than anyone can know. Love is greater than the sum of its parts.

Love is a mystery, as are most of the truly profound experiences in life. Robert Farrar Capon refers to mystery as "our oldest, truest home."[1] That certainly describes love as well.

People uncomfortable with mystery have little hope of experiencing the heights of love, or the depths of faith. In Christianity, both faith and love are essential. But neither develops apart from mystery. The apostle Paul refers to messengers of the gospel as "stewards of God's mysteries" (1 Cor. 4:1).

A person who doesn't appreciate mystery likely misunderstands the nature of relationships—relationships between people and relationships between people and God. We cannot be reasoned or debated into intimate love. In relation to God, neither faith nor love is born of passionate, argumentative apologetics.

Most intimate relationships defy solely rational descriptions. Loving relationships are filled with mystery. Spiritually, people are loved into a relationship with God—a relationship that can be affirmed only by faith and expressed only by demonstrations of more love.

The Mystery of Prayer

Not only is mystery a trait of true love, mystery is a characteristic of authentic prayer. Understanding prayer is not a prerequisite to praying any more than explanations of love are required prior to loving. Individuals spontaneously, almost instinctively, embrace the experience of love or prayer (or both) before they realize what is happening. In the midst of a life-threatening crisis, a self-declared agnostic shouts, "God, help us!" A confirmed recluse meets a person with whom she falls desperately in love. Later these folks shake their heads in disbelief—not disbelief about the authenticity of the experience, but disbelief about their previous blindness to a mystery which they now recognize as a stunning reality.

When we view prayer as mystery, as communion between lovers, many of the most common questions about prayer suddenly seem irrelevant—or redundant. What good does it do to spend time with the person you love? How does love between two lovers grow as a result of shared experiences? Why is sitting on a park bench in silence with the person you love so much more meaningful than jogging five miles alone?

Ask two lovers: "Do you get anything out of just being with each other?"

"You must be kidding!" The lovers are obviously dumbfounded. "We love each other. There is nothing we would rather do than be together. We want to share our joys, hurts, concerns, needs, failures, successes, hopes, and dreams. We enjoy being together. We're in love! What else can we say?"

If prayer is communion between two lovers, questions about its benefits and how it works—if it really does work—get swallowed up in mystery—the mystery of love. God and the pray-er are in love with each other. Each desires unbroken contact and open sharing with the other. Enjoying communion with one another is all that either lover needs as an explanation of the value of prayer. That is the beauty—and the mystery—of being in love.

Risking Vulnerability

Falling in love is scary. Growing in love is scarier still. It requires openness between lovers, complete openness.

Nothing can be hidden or held back. Each allows the other to see who he is and what she is like, sharing innermost thoughts, desires, secrets, confessions, hopes, beliefs, and requests.

Radical openness—a tough assignment in itself—creates vulnerability, which does not come naturally or easy for anybody. Security looks more attractive than risk; playing it safe is more alluring than ventures into the unknown. Most of us find greater comfort in building walls than in opening windows through which others can see and understand us. Issues of ease aside, however, an enjoyment of mature love and experiences of real intimacy are completely out of the question apart from a risk of vulnerability—whether in relation to other people or in relation to God.

Arguments against Vulnerability

A sizable segment of our society argues against the development of vulnerability. Conventional wisdom counsels people to play life close to the vest in every situation: "Never reveal your true emotions. Keep a stiff upper lip. Don't trust anybody else enough to let them see inside your heart and mind." In other words, don't risk being hurt.

Following this advice produces rigid people—individuals who fear that any demonstration of great joy or expression of profound sorrow might leave them open to criticism or abuse. Blandness and mediocrity become behavioral norms.

Individuals dedicated to living a cautious, uptight lifestyle get together with other people socially but never allow themselves to become close to others personally—they talk incessantly with almost everybody but only infrequently (if ever) experience communion with anybody; and they claim numerous acquaintances while lamenting a lack of any real friends. Sadly, such people become so adept at hiding their true selves from others that eventually they don't even know who they are. Worst of all, overly self-protective persons develop a superficial spirituality in which they value a relationship with God but refuse to include honesty, commitment, and communion within that relationship.

Issues of Vulnerability

Anybody can understand most people's resistance to vulnerability. Openness means letting our defenses down. A vulnerable person lays himself completely open to be hurt or helped. Every shared thought and every intimate conversation sets up the possibility of affirmation or rejection, elation or dejection, joy or sadness. However, if we never risk rejection, we never know the joy of affirmation. Without vulnerability, intimacy never develops and, thus, love never matures.

Frequently a person says to me, "I've been hurt for the last time. I'm never going to get close enough to someone to fall in love and get hurt again." Such reasoning makes sense, but it represents a life-draining, starkly deadening decision. Happiness and sadness, joy and grief, and hope and despair come from the same place in the heart. People who steel themselves against pain also shield themselves from joy.

Self-protection blocks the way to vulnerability and obstructs movement toward a life of love.[2] That explains why Jesus so often instructed a would-be disciple to give up something in order to follow God: "Go, sell what you own, and give the money to the poor, and . . . and come, follow me" (Mark 10:21). The same truth prompted Jesus' call for "self-denial" from his disciples: "If any want to become my followers, let them deny themselves and take up their cross and follow me" (Mark 8:34; Matt. 16:24;

Luke 9:23). Jesus wanted God's followers to remove from their lives all barriers to the vulnerability necessary for a development of intimate love.

Here, again, it makes perfectly good sense—humanly speaking—to resist Jesus' demand. "If I give away everything, what will I have to fall back on if things go bad?" "Do I really want to open myself to such a strong possibility of hurt? Isn't that just asking for trouble?" But, more is involved here than sound reasoning. Only through a willful acceptance of vulnerability can an individual demonstrate the kind of open-ended commitment to Jesus that makes discipleship possible. And who can put a price tag on a loving relationship with Jesus?

Another vulnerability issue in a loving relationship—many would say "the most important vulnerability issue"—revolves around the possibility (or necessity) of change. A lover who entrusts decisions about the future to her beloved faces the distinct possibility of having to make major changes in her life. For people who find security and comfort in maintaining the status quo, this very real potential for change stands as an imposing hindrance to any pursuit of intimacy. Some individuals simply cannot tolerate anyone else being in charge of their lives—not even momentarily, not even a loved one, not even God.

Vulnerability is to intimate love what oxygen is to fire. Without one, you don't have the other. Conversely, where one is present, the other is sure to be found as well.

Vulnerability and Prayer

A willingness to be searched and known by God pervades meaningful prayer. So does running the risk of being changed. As one student of love observes, "The kind of communication which is the lifeblood of love will require me to get in touch with my most sensitive feelings and my most buried thoughts, and to share these in the frightening act of self-disclosure."[3]

Meaningful prayer nurtures and is nurtured by vulnerability. A strange thing happens. At the very moment we set security aside in favor of risk, we discover an even greater security—a God-given security—which lessens our sense of risk. God's love (which precedes our love) assures us of understanding, acceptance, grace, forgiveness, and encouragement. From the beginning of our communion with God, we are freed to open ourselves to God unconditionally.

Even at that, though, many people approach God tentatively, cautiously testing the waters of spirituality. That's all right, as long as communion with God begins. The more openness to God a person risks, the more certain that individual becomes of God's love, the more freedom is experienced, and the more profound will be the intimacy which develops between that individual and God.

Warnings against vulnerability trade on the assumption that where a potential for hurt exists, the reality of hurt will be experienced. And, they may be right. But look at the total picture. Hurt is not all that comes from the vulnerability of love. So do greater love and immeasurable joy.

Models of Vulnerability

A New Testament character named Zacchaeus serves as a kind of patron saint of vulnerability. This diminutive government official possessed such a passion to see Jesus that he would do anything, even sacrifice professional and personal dignity by climbing a tree, to catch a glimpse of the itinerant preacher. You can almost hear onlookers poking fun at him. But Zacchaeus wanted to see Jesus. Zacchaeus up a tree embodies vulnerability.

And was it worthwhile! As a result of Zaccheus' venture into vulnerability, this man not only saw Jesus but met God for a meal and became one of God's followers. Look what happened: passion prompted vulnerability in Zaccheus. That vulnerability created opportunities for growth in love. Devotion developed and acts of loving service followed. Please don't miss the equation: no love, no vulnerability; no vulnerability, no strengthened love.

Stories of love-inspired vulnerability fill the pages of the Bible. As a result of his love for God, Abraham risked losing all his security, lovingly ventured into the unknown, and developed an intimate friendship with God. Similarly, Noah opened himself to public ridicule as he obeyed the God he loved, the God who saved him in a time of crisis. A young Jewish maiden named Mary risked her personal reputation as well as her physical well-being in order to obey God. From that vulnerability sprang the Incarnation of Love.

Not even God can separate love from vulnerability. The revelation of God's love for the world resulted in the crucifixion of Jesus. However, that was not the end of God's love. Out of the cruel hurt which people inflicted upon Jesus came unforgettable insights into the durable, powerful nature of God's love. God offered forgiveness and salvation to those who caused the hurt.

Intimate relationships cannot develop apart from the risk of vulnerability. God could not love without vulner-ability. Neither can we.

This discussion of vulnerability reveals a serious flaw in our otherwise helpful metaphor. A love affair with God differs dramatically from a love affair with another person. We always can count on God. Always! A human being may surprise us with betrayal, hurt us by failure to keep a promise or sustain a commitment, or devastate our trust by acts of infidelity. Not God! Lovers of God need never fear betrayal, infidelity, or desertion by God.

Lovers of God open the entirety of their beings to God after the pattern of any true lover, including God the Lover. Prayer arises out of that openness. We risk looking and sounding like fools as we set inhibitions aside to voice our enthusiastic, exultant praise to God. Our spirits tremble as we allow God to look into our doubts and observe our weaknesses through our confessions. It's strange that we become so uneasy given the fact that God already knows all we reveal, but we do. We hold our breaths, unable to anticipate the consequence of the commitment in which we say to God, "Not our wills, but Your will be done." It's scary talk, but it's real prayer—the language of vulnerability. It is not without cost. But neither is it without great promise.

The Promise of Vulnerability

The most significant moments in a person's prayer life usually occur when an individual feels completely naked before God—stripped of all pretense, devoid of any masks, honest about sins, straightforward concerning needs, all defensive shields laid down, open to traveling in new directions. With deep bruises, embarrassing fears, and sensitive spots in the soul fully exposed, a person joyously discovers the depths of God's comfort, the wonder of God's leadership, and the power of God's healing love.

Nurturing Intimacy

Love leads to intimacy. In turn, experiences of intimacy nurture greater love. Lovers view intimacy as both a desirable goal toward which their love should move and a source of the strength required to sustain that movement. Prayer emerges from intimacy between God and an individual as well as contributes to even more intimacy within their love affair.

The meaning of the word *intimacy* points to the nature of an intimate relationship. Our English word comes from a superlative form of the Latin term *inter* which means "within, inner, or innermost" (*intima*). An intimate relationship is one in which the inmost dimensions of two lovers' lives engage and touch each other.[4] Nurturing intimacy with God requires lovingly opening the depth of our beings to God in a process aimed at experiencing the true nature of God's Being.

Though most all lovers project intimacy as a major goal of their relationship, failures in intimacy far outnumber successes. Intimacy does not develop easily or quickly.

Closeness and Intimacy

Sometimes people mistake closeness for intimacy, but the two are not the same. Intimacy cannot develop without closeness, but closeness can be experienced apart from intimacy.[5] Two people can feel close to each other because they enjoy being together. The same can be said of an individual's relationship to God. Intimacy between lovers, however, involves much more than being in each other's presence.

Intimacy requires us to know ourselves as well as the persons whose company we enjoy (the persons to whom we feel close). I can be close to another person without ever coming to grips with who I am or allowing the other person any significant insight into my identity. If I am ever to share intimacy with that other person, though, I have to not only know myself but allow the other person to know what I know about myself—a very difficult assignment.

Typically, we explore our own natures only in private, if at all. We may even do all our introspection in complete seclusion, guarding against anybody else knowing what we find out about ourselves. Understanding myself requires me to answer demanding questions such as: Who am I really? What are my dreams? What are my goals? What are my strengths and weaknesses? What is the nature of my faith or the reason for an absence of faith? What makes me mad or sad, discontented or happy? What do I look for in other people? What do I fear? Whom do I love? It's hard enough to answer these questions honestly when alone. Answering them in the presence of another person or before God may appear virtually impossible. But it's not.

Nurturing intimacy—with another person or with God—involves serious self-exploration in the presence of our lover. We risk truthfully seeing ourselves—the good and the bad, promises and problems, successes and failures—while in the presence of the one we love more than anyone else. What a frightening thought!

Needless to say, people find avoiding intimacy to be much easier than achieving it. Nurturing intimacy demands effort, courage, and patience. Escaping intimacy requires far less strength and character.

Ways to Avoid Intimacy

Specialists who study relationships identify specific means by which people avoid intimacy.[6] Each of these defensive patterns of behavior can hinder intimacy with God as effectively as in interpersonal relations.

Withdrawal. One popular tactic for avoiding intimacy involves withdrawal. By avoiding public worship, prohibiting periods of private meditation, and ignoring impulses to pray, some people never confront the demand (which is really a privilege) to know themselves in relation to God.

Ironically, such people usually reach a point where they complain about "the distance of God" or "the absence of God" from their lives when they have been running as fast as possible to get away from even the slightest brush with God.

Personal Neediness. Some people avoid intimacy by practicing personal neediness. Employing this strategy in relation to God, an individual allows his prayers to contain nothing but requests. Each of his prayers sounds like a "Christmas wish list": "God, please give me . . . ; God, supply me with . . . ; God, I badly need . . . ." When speaking to God, the pray-er carefully steers clear of reflective or introspective statements; therefore, intimacy cannot develop.

Self-righteousness. Any possibility for intimacy can be shut down by self-righteousness. For some individuals, a need to be right far outweighs a desire to be loved. Such people never confess a mistake, admit a sin, or acknowledge a weakness in relation to God (or to anyone else). They seem incapable of the very kind of honesty about themselves which is a prerequisite to intimacy. All of their prayers sound like monologues offered for God's enlightenment.

Rigidity. Opportunities for intimacy are destroyed by rigidity also. Persons who refuse to acknowledge any view of themselves other than their own close themselves off from intimate relations. Intimacy with God develops when we see who we are and where we are in relation to God as well as how God can change us. Obviously, if we refuse to look at ourselves realistically, we never even recognize a need to change, much less open ourselves to the possibility of change. Personal rigidity functions as an impregnable fortress which shuts out intimacy of any kind—even intimacy with God.

Promises of Intimacy

Our reservations about intimacy are perfectly understandable. However, even a slight understanding of the joy of an intimate relationship makes a risk of intimacy more attractive. Experiencing intimacy means living in a loving relationship in which you know yourself, you freely reveal this knowledge to your lover, you fully know who your lover is, and you both realize the incredible grace of full acceptance. Within an intimate relationship, you discover responsibilities, enjoy attentiveness, identify personality dynamics, explore feelings, study how to serve as a conduit of love, learn how to let go in surrender, and work at the best way to communicate with your lover.[7]

The Work of Intimacy

Intimacy does not develop automatically. It requires work, but not just any kind of work. Nurturing intimacy is more an art than a science. Intimacy issues focus on being rather than doing.[8] Achieving intimacy requires nothing short of a commitment of life.

Communication nurtures intimacy. However, intimacy is more than communication.[9] Experiencing intimacy with God embraces not only times filled with words of prayer but moments when sighs replace words and silence snuffs out all audible expressions. Intimacy between lovers intensifies amid gaps in verbal communication—in times of frustration when feelings refuse to be reduced to words and in situations where every attempt to speak intelligently ends in failure.

In an intimate relationship with God, we sense a challenge to become all that God created us to be. But that is not simple. Affirmation and encouraging love from God remain constant. However, conflicting desires tug at our souls. In one instant, we want to look at ourselves honestly, while in another instant we desire to be less preoccupied with ourselves. With a surge of excitement, we resolve to take charge of our lives. Then comes a passionate desire to surrender ourselves to God.

Personal surrender forms a foundation for healthy closeness and intimacy—especially in a relationship with God. Strangely, we experience the greatest degree of self-fulfillment by overcoming selfishness. That is not double-talk. We become most fully ourselves by owning up to who we are and surrendering ourselves to God.[10]

Authentic intimacy deepens the mystery of love while increasing our willingness to risk vulnerability in relation to our lover. Intimacy also contributes to the enjoyment of liberty. Knowing that I can be who I am freely and fully in the presence of my Beloved instills within me the truest freedom that humankind can experience.[11]

Enjoying Liberty

Nowhere do we enjoy more freedom than in relationship with one who accepts us for who we are and loves us beyond measure—namely God. In fellowship with our Lover, we do not have to worry about saying or doing something which will prompt rejection. To paraphrase the apostle Paul, there is nothing in all creation that will separate us from God the Lover (Rom. 8:39).

Communion with a devoted lover is one of life's greatest treasures. Thoughts flow lucidly. No emotion has to be repressed. Honest questions are in order. Words need not be measured meticulously. In prayer, we claim the freedom birthed within a love affair and rejoice in an assurance that free expression between lovers contributes to greater love.

73

Freedom as Choice

Love makes freedom possible among lovers. However, that liberty must be claimed. Our realization of freedom depends upon our choice of freedom.

Several years ago, Ernest Campbell preached a wonderful sermon entitled "Locked in a Room with Open Doors." Campbell's intriguing sermon title came from a comment in Hans Sachs' story about a young man who had a dreadful fear of open doors. This fellow's older brother, weary of his sibling's strange malady and eager to break his bad habit, finally threatened him, "One day I will lock you up in a room with all the doors open."[12]

What a terrific insight into freedom resides in the image of this boy locked in a room with open doors. His bondage resulted from an inner condition, not from a lack of freedom. All that stood between this young fellow and liberty was a personal choice—a decision to experience freedom.

God wills for us to live in liberty. Indeed, freedom accompanies God's gift of love. God calls us to liberty: "You were called to freedom" the apostle Paul wrote (Gal. 5:13). But we have to accept God's offer. God will not force liberty upon us. We can enjoy a life of freedom only if we choose liberty rather than bondage. It's each person's decision.

Any sense of bondage we experience in prayer has its source inside us. God grants us complete freedom to pray as we need to pray. No specific words are required, no particular structure, no one emotion. God desires to hear our praise, confessions, intercessions, and petitions in whatever manner most honestly conveys our thoughts and feelings.

Interestingly, the word *freedom* comes to us through old Celtic roots meaning "dear." In earlier days, people kin to the master of a house by blood were considered "dear" or "free," in contrast to slaves within the dwelling. The word *choice* meant "try." So, a free choice was a "dear try."[13] Choosing to claim the freedom offered by a lover is a "dear try," a cherished risk.

Love and freedom belong together. The love within a love affair produces freedom, respects freedom, and nurtures freedom among the lovers just as the freedom within a love affair motivates lovers to express love, strengthen love, and focus love. Both involve risks and require choices. Real prayer represents a "dear try"—a free choice which embraces a big risk—to set before God our identity, concerns, needs, sins, and thankfulness.

A Fear of Freedom

Strange as it may seem, some people prefer bondage to freedom. They would rather react than act, conform than create. Obeying someone else's orders about what to do and say in every situation relieves them from having to think, make evaluations, take risks, exercise discretion, and wrestle with personal responsibility. Sadly, though, self-chosen servitude also blunts the potential for a person to grow in love.

I know individuals who live in bondage to the expectations of other people, fearing to exercise their God-given freedom to be themselves, not wanting to be caught up in conflict or to risk rejection. Pleasing others seems more important to these individuals than honest expressions of their own convictions. Similarly, they value security much more than liberty, preferring to be safe rather than free if a choice between the two must be made. These people successfully avoid controversy, disagreements, and failures, not rocking any boats relationally—even if that requires repressing convictions, silencing judgments, and, thus, compromising responsible freedom. Internally, though, they come to despise themselves, hating their reticence as well their lack of honesty, courage, and confidence.

Growth in love cannot occur apart from lovers freely expressing themselves to each other. So what if they disagree at times or even argue? How else will they get to know one another? Only when enjoying liberty do lovers learn to exercise the greatest gifts of love: understanding, forgiveness, reconciliation, and renewal.

Knowing full well that we may fear the precious gift of freedom, God fills us with a love which sets aside that fear ("Perfect love casts out fear," John wrote in 1 John 4:18). Thus, we "struggle through the maze of needs, desires, fears, hurts, angers, lusts, shames, sadnesses, and loves to choose those which most represent who we are."[14] Then, we freely and confidently share who we are with the one we love, the one who loves us, knowing that such sharing enriches our love and strengthens the relationship.

Fear is not incompatible with prayer. Sometimes fear seems inevitable in prayer. On numerous occasions I have repeated to God a virtual litany of personal fears—fear of failure, fear of unemployment, fear of controversy, fear of exclusion. However, the very prayer which begins with a confession of fear steadily leads to the Lover in whose presence fear recedes and freedom emerges.

Commitment and Liberty

An unfortunate misunderstanding equates liberty with an undisciplined, irresponsible lifestyle. According to popular misrepresentations, free people always get their way and do everything they want to do. Wrong! A meaningful love affair could never even develop in that situation, much less provide freedom for personal and relational growth.

Within a love affair, love produces liberty. Liberty makes commitment possible. Commitment enhances both the love and the liberty which lovers enjoy.

Commitment—in no sense the opposite of freedom—represents one of the highest expressions of freedom. When without pressure, threats, and coercion, I freely decide to give myself to another in love, I touch the core of liberty as well as the essence of life. Commitment literally means "to put oneself with"; it's a choice, a "dear try." When I put myself with another, choosing to live in a covenant relationship, I exercise my personal freedom and prepare myself to know an even greater freedom.

The only authentic prayer is a free one—a prayer I choose to pray. And the highest reach of my freedom in prayer comes not so much when I express anger to God, raise questions for God, or declare doubts before God as when I make a commitment to God. At the very moment I seem to be giving up freedom in order to live out a commitment, I discover more love and freedom.

One of my favorite prayers captures the essence of the relationship between love, freedom, and commitment.

> *Help us so to know you [God]*
> *that we may truly love you,*
> *so to love you*
> *that we may truly serve you,*
> whose service is perfect freedom.[15]

ઽ

PART THREE

Love commands a vast army of moods.
Diane Ackerman, *A Natural History of Love*

Speaking Lovingly to God

CHAPTER SIX

Dishonesty is the enemy of intimacy . . .
Dishonesty creates distance.

Frank Pittman, *Private Lies*

PRAYING HONESTLY

Intimacy requires honesty. Dishonesty halts the development of love and destroys love affairs.

Love and truth go together. Try to tear the two apart in a love affair and you compromise both love and truth as well as destroy the lovers' relationship. Communion which strengthens the bond between lovers depends upon the presence of both love and truth.

Telling the truth is not always easy, not even for lovers. Truth does not always comfort, please, or delight the person who hears it, not even when spoken with love. Often statements of truth disturb, upset, anger, or cause hurt. Nevertheless, truth-telling remains an essential ingredient in durable, loving relationships.

Only honesty provides a solid foundation upon which lovers can construct an enduring trust. Distortions, cover-ups, deception, and lies completely destroy trust and devastate relationships. And when trust between lovers disappears, so does any possibility of growth in a covenant relationship. Faced by a particularly bothersome situation, neither lover may like the content of a specific truth which needs to be shared—"I didn't keep my promise to you"; "I have done something that will disappoint you." However, both know that the health and durability of their love for each other cannot survive without honesty.

Many therapists argue that the dishonesty which usually accompanies infidelity takes a much heavier toll on a relationship than the specific actions involved. Lovers can overcome virtually all forms of betrayal, even adultery, if honesty between them survives. However, an absence of honesty virtually assures a lack of forgiveness, reconciliation, and a reestablishment of trust. Noted psychiatrist and family therapist Frank Pittman asserts, "There is no truth that is as destructive as any lie."[1]

God delights in truth. In the Old Testament we read, "You desire truth in the inward being" (Ps. 51:6); "Thus says the LORD . . . love truth" (Zech. 8:19). In the New Testament, Jesus revealed the God of truth, identifying Himself as "truth" (John 14:6), and commissioned God's followers to live guided by the Spirit of truth (John 16:13).

Not uncommonly, early pietists referred to God as Truth in their prayers. Julian of Norwich confessed, "Good LORD, I can see that you are real truth."[2] Augustine declared to God, "Truth is nothing else but thou thyself."[3] Thomas à Kempis addressed God saying, "O Truth, that God art, make me one with Thee in perfect charity."[4]

Freedom in Honesty

Much more important than calling God "Truth" is speaking to God truthfully. Prayer consists of telling God the truth. But many of us have trouble at this point.

Sometimes frustration, resentment, doubts, and anger so dominate our spirits that we hesitate to tell God our true feelings. However, God knows we experience difficult times and face stressful situations in our spiritual pilgrimages. We need not attempt to avoid God or to hide our sentiments from God at such moments. God invites honesty from us in every prayer we offer—valuing statements of honest doubt far more than dishonest confessions of faith and welcoming outbursts of honest anger rather than superficial declarations of feigned adoration. We deceive only ourselves by thinking we can hide truth from God.

Personal Liberty

I remember when I first realized the full significance of speaking honestly to God. A freedom in prayer developed unlike anything I had known before—and a terrific sense of release. I knew that anything and everything could be said to a lover without any fear of a response that was not loving. And I saw God as the Ultimate Lover.

Oh, I had never lied to God or assumed I could fool God. However, many times in my prayers I simply remained silent about experiences which made me feel shame or guilt before God. I was not dishonest with God, just not totally honest. Perhaps I foolishly thought that if I did not mention these disturbing matters to God we both would forget them. Of course, that was not the case. The experiences and their subsequent emotions which I refused to bring to God's attention ate away at my soul.

Even a painful prayer about honesty became a stepping-stone to liberty. I discovered liberating dimensions of God's truth by being truthful with God:

Honesty is so difficult, God.
Even in a church building constructed to strengthen integrity, I have a problem with honesty—shifting back and forth in my soul as if shuffling my feet, grappling with thoughts in my mind as if clearing my throat.

83

I am concerned about self-respect. I don't want others to know me like I know myself or to think I have sins to confess. Pretense is a good defense against self-revelation.

And, God, what in heaven's name would You think if You knew I harbor doubts as well as faith, I sometimes question the wisdom of the gospel, I suspicion whether or not anyone really can make it in this world by loving, serving, forgiving, and praying?

Of course, You already know. And already knowing, You understand me. You accept me. You love me. You will help me, even during my title-fights with honesty.

O God, please help me keep an honest relationship with You and speak with You honestly. I want to be set free by the truth. And, You know I'm trying. The bondage of deception still rubs me uncomfortably, but, with Your help, I am moving toward liberty with integrity.

Thank You God, thank You so much, for knowing me, loving me, enabling me to say what I need to say, and promising to stay with me not only until all is said and done but even after all is said and done.

My efforts and my thanks, I offer in the Name of the One called Truth.

Personal Safety

When a troubled person comes to me for counseling, in our first session together I often say, "This is a safe place. You can be completely honest here without any dread that I will attack you. Tell me what's going on inside you." These words reflect my understanding of the nature of prayer. Prayer is a safe place. God my Lover wants me to speak of the storms in my soul, to talk about my situation honestly and specifically. Knowing that God loves me, I can bare my soul with the confidence that nothing I say will cause God to stop loving me or deny me the joy of forgiveness and redemption.

Intimate conversations with lovers embrace the good and the evil in our lives—accomplishments over which we rejoice and failures about which we grieve. Lovers both laugh and cry together as a result of speaking to each other with an honesty which strengthens their intimacy. In the process of such truth-telling, we come to a greater awareness of true communion, deeper love, and fantastic freedom. Prayer is communion between two lovers.

Not long after I came to a full recognition of God as Lover and began to ponder the implications of this reality for honesty, I started a prayer saying,

Finally!

At long last, I am in a relationship and a conversation in which I can be totally honest. I am so weary of surface emotions, meaningless gibberish, and superficial interaction.

God, You know. You know these situations and hear the words which I speak to fill them.

Unburdening my soul brought a rush of relief and courage to keep speaking honestly.

I am worried to death about how to meet this month's budget. I feel absolutely frantic over decisions which I need to make before I am ready.

A friend has hurt me badly. I want to run, hide, and protect myself from more pain. But when an acquaintance asks me how I am doing, I smile and say, "Just fine."

I'm not fine, God! I am tired of faking enthusiasm, saying what I don't mean, and compromising my personal integrity to gain social acceptance.

Never had prayer meant more to me than in this moment. Beginning to pray honestly felt like lancing a painful boil. Suddenly pent-up infections of the soul flowed freely to the surface. Hurt accompanied my confession, but it was different. I felt the hurt which precedes healing, not the hurt which signals the approach of death. No sooner had I concluded my prayer than I sensed a surprising desire to pray again.

Doubts and Devotion

Not only do expressions of doubt and exclamations of devotion have a place in prayer, these often come from the same pray-er. The father of an epileptic boy healed by Jesus said to the Savior, "I believe; help my unbelief!"(Mark 9:24). This remarkably truthful statement serves as a prototype for honest prayer.

Two persons engaged in a love affair with each other know both the glory of surging devotion and the aggravation of nagging doubts. "I know you say you will accept me for who I am," one says, "but I can't help but wonder if you really will." "I understand," comes the response, "I love you so much, but I have serious weak spots in my life which cause me to doubt that you could continue to love me."

Devotion no more shuts down doubts than doubts prevent growth in devotion. "Christian faith is a principle of questioning and struggle before it becomes a principle of certitude and peace," Thomas Merton asserted. The well-known monk went on to declare, "One has to doubt and reject everything else in order to believe firmly in Christ, and after one has begun to believe, one's faith must be tested and purified."[5]

Typically, our devotion to God reaches its greatest depths only after we have survived tumultuous spiritual storms and battled tortuous doubts. God understands. Many of God's boldest servants emerged from soulful skirmishes with God in which they screamed their doubts and struggled with faith. God welcomes a devotion unafraid of honest questioning.

Philip Yancey explains that "God . . . desires not the clinging, helpless love of a child who has no choice, but the mature, freely given love of a lover."[6] We declare our devotion to God not because we have no other option, but because, faced with many demands upon our affections, we have chosen to love God with all our hearts, souls, and minds. We pray to God not because we have to but because we want to; we desire to be in constant contact with our Lover.

Back in the eleventh century, Anselm of Canterbury beautifully blended his concerns about doubts with his desire for understanding and his will toward greater devotion. Anselm prayed, "Since, LORD, it is you who gives understanding to our faith, grant me to understand, as far as you think fit, that you are as we believe, and that you are what we believe you to be."[7]

Complaints and Convictions

Honest communion with God consists of both convictions and complaints. "I love you, O LORD, my strength" the psalmist prayed (18:1); the same psalmist who complained, "O LORD . . . Your arrows have sunk into me, and your hand has come down on me" (38:1–2).

In many instances, the very convictions about God's greatness which give rise to prayers of exaltation also prompt complaints to God. Meditations on the nature of the Divine Lover bring into focus God's awesome power, disdain of evil, opposition to oppression, passion for justice, and relentless mercy. These insights into the character of God occur, however, amid a proliferation of evil, oppression, injustice, and hostility in our world. Something seems out of kilter. Our understanding of the nature of God clashes with our awareness of the condition of the world.

"If God is all-powerful love, surely God can do something about the lovelessness rampant all around us." "But, dare we say that to God?" We ask ourselves. "Should we complain to God?" The answer is yes; yes, by all means, if a complaint to God reflects the honest will of our hearts.

A Spiritual Brother

Observe the piety of Jeremiah. While the Babylonian army besieged the city of Jerusalem, this prophet prayed to God. He began with praise, "It is you who made the heavens and the earth by your great power . . . Nothing is too hard for you." But then, thinking of the situation in which he was praying, Jeremiah's prayer of praise turned into a strong complaint: "The siege-ramps have been cast up against the city to take it, and the city, faced with sword, famine, and pestilence, has been given into the hands of the Chaldeans" (Jer. 32:17–24).

Whoever heard of a love affair in which the lovers did not exchange complaints? Our Lover, God, wants to hear our troublesome complaints as well as our comforting convictions.

Periodically, I unload my complaints before God.

God, I don't understand.

> You love mercy but tolerate meanness. You call us to peace and allow violence to rule the streets.

> You demand purity of Your people while Your world gets dirtier and dirtier.

> You praise goodness while allowing evil people to succeed.

> If You were not the majestic, powerful, merciful Lover I know You to be, I could better understand what's going on.

> But, You are God!

Such a prayer does not come easily for me. It seems so audacious. But the motivation behind it is the honesty appropriate between lovers.

Reading the words of Jeremiah, the seventh-century B.C. prophet, reminds me of a roller coaster. From a high point of emotionally voiced convictions, the prophet's prayers suddenly plunge into complaints. Or from the depths of despair, we follow the prophet's slow but steady ascendancy (clack, clack, clack) to another pinnacle. Within the short expanse of twenty verses, the prophet declares, "The steadfast love of the LORD never ceases, his mercies never come to an end; . . . great is your faithfulness" (Lam. 3:22–23) and "You have wrapped yourself with anger and pursued us; . . . You have wrapped yourself with a cloud so that no prayer can pass through" (Lam. 3:43–44). Jeremiah recognizes the ambivalence of his dilemma and expresses appreciation for God's attentiveness to both his convictions and complaints, "Righteous art thou, O LORD, when I complain to thee" (Jer. 12:1, RSV).

Who has not been in such a situation? Jeremiah is our spiritual brother. In difficult moments I have said to God, "I know You fill us with sensitivity and teach us to care. But I am tired of sensitivity and caring. It seems like I can never rest because another situation needs attention. I wish I could just turn away. But, You won't let me do it. And, God, the disappointments which come with abuses or rejections of care are almost more than I can stand. I wish You had not made me this way."

Actually, complaining to God can represent as much trust in God and love for God as declaring convictions. God loves us with understanding and an abiding appreciation for honesty. Besides, God, too, has complaints.

A Divine Complaint

Philip Yancey envisions God going to a counselor who says to God, "Tell me how you really feel." God eagerly responds, "I'll tell you how I feel!" Then comes a recitation of complaints: "I feel like a jilted lover. I found my lover thin and wasted, abused, but I brought her home and made her beauty shine. . . . I lavish on her gifts and love. And yet she forsakes me . . . worse than a prostitute, she pays people to have sex with her. I feel betrayed, abandoned, cuckolded."[8] Yancey concludes that love complicates God's life just as it does every life.

True love births complaints and convictions. True lovers find a way to express both in a manner which nurtures trust and intimacy between them.

Questions and Affirmations

Affirming a lover comes as naturally as breathing. With sheer delight, we eagerly tell the loves in our lives, "You are the most wonderful person I have ever known"; "You do everything just right;" "You're beautiful!" Questioning, though, is another matter—especially if it creates the possibility of a quarrel. Some well-intentioned people wrongfully argue that questions which challenge a lover should go unvoiced in the interest of maintaining peace. But authentic love finds no pleasure in peace constructed from cowardly silence and supported by repressed inquiries. Love can grow to new depths as a result of honest questioning and controversial conversations. But deception, repression, and dishonesty destroy love.

Most of the spiritual giants described in the Bible contended with, debated, and questioned God as well as affirmed, adored, and praised God. Abraham, an early patriarch known for his faith, quizzed God: "Will You indeed sweep away the righteous with the wicked? . . . Shall not the Judge of all the earth do what is just?" (Gen. 18:23–25). Later, the prophet Habakkuk screamed to the heavens, "O Lord, how long shall I cry for help, and you will not listen?" (1:2). Similarly, the psalmist asked, "How long, O Lord? Will you forget me forever? How long will you hide your face from me?" (13:1). Even Jesus—the embodiment of faithful love, the epitome of a faithful lover—voiced this question in God's greatest hour of need: "My God, my God, why have you forsaken me?" (Mark 15:34).

Not all questions set before God reflect the same spirit or purpose. Through the centuries, lovers of God have questioned God for a variety of reasons. Surrounded by adversaries charging God with a lack of interest in those who pray, the author of Psalm 10 complains to God: "Why, O Lord, do you stand far off? Why do you hide yourself in times of trouble?"(10:1). Baffled by conditions he saw around him in the eighth century, Alcuin of York asked God for an explanation, "Why do you allow wars and massacres on earth? By what mysterious judgment do you allow innocent people to be cruelly slaughtered?"[9] Motivated by his desperate desire for God's assistance in being a better person, John of the Cross pleadingly queried God, "Why are you waiting? Why do you delay in pouring out the love for which I yearn?"[10] Trying to make sense of the hardships in his life, Dag Hammarskjöld questioned God with obvious devotion: "Did'st Thou give me this inescapable loneliness so that it would be easier for me to give Thee all?"[11] Perplexed by God's love for her, despite disobedience and weaknesses, Catherine of Genoa asked, "Lord, why do you illumine a soul so rank—an enemy who continually flees from you, an obstinate, sensual soul?"[12]

I have done my share of questioning God, explaining to God that my "sole reason for pursuing answers to these questions is to embrace new convictions while strengthening old ones."[13] But the motivation behind my questions fails to ease the pain with which I raise them or my eagerness to be rid of them.

Why are so many folks fearful of freedom? Can faith exist without nagging doubts? ... Why can spring, with its budding flowers and greening grass, not arrive apart from killer tornadoes? Will we ever be able to enjoy a parade of celebration without the tormenting fear of betrayal or assassination?"[14]

God welcomes honest questions. Such inquiries do not silence honest affirmations of God. Sometimes a prayerful question, like one raised by the Puritan poet Anne Bradstreet, conveys powerful affirmation: "Why should I live but to Thy praise?"[15] In a moving confession, Philip Jebb articulated the spirit which properly dominates both the affirmations and questions which we direct to God, "Lord, I confess that you are good, and that to you all gentleness and love belong. . . . When there comes upon me the great pain of my heart and head, it is to you that I must look, and the look must be one of love, not reproach."[16]

Personal Needs and Social Concerns

Speaking honestly to God about ourselves leads to speaking honestly to God about the world around us, and vice versa. The prophet Isaiah's well-known lament, "Woe is me," complemented—not contradicted or diverted attention from—his statement about society: "I live among a people of unclean lips"(6:5). God seeks our honest assessment of how things are with us and with the people among whom we live.

Barriers to Being Honest with God

Our defense mechanisms make honest statements of self-revelation difficult. "Don't let anybody see your faults, hide your weaknesses, cover up your anxieties, stay silent about your anger, and keep a calm demeanor at all times," counsel self acclaimed experts on personal success and social acceptance. Wrong! This flawed, though popular, advice promotes deception, a natural enemy of love. Guarding against any instance of negative self-disclosure ultimately results in destructive self-deception and the outlandish assumption that we can deceive God.

Difficult though it may be, only honest self-disclosure in prayer reveals love—thus pleasing God and helping us. I have to work constantly at such honesty. Here is an example:

> God, I don't feel like praying.
>
> I know I need the communion with You, but I sense a void, a chasm, between us. Surely, You understand.
>
> Or, maybe You don't. During this weekend I have been watching football and baseball, cleaning the house, working and playing outside—enjoying life.
>
> The thought of prayer brings into focus a lot of serious stuff and, frankly, I have more than enough serious business to deal with next week.
>
> Right now I don't feel like praying.

Speaking truthfully to God about myself ranks among the most difficult of spiritual exercises for me. But, also among the most fulfilling and freeing. I have to work hard at this kind of prayer, but, in retrospect, I never regret either the labor or its fruits.

Aids to Being Honest with God

Reading or hearing the honesty with which other people have spoken to God helps me be more honest about myself. Henri Nouwen prayed, "O dear Lord, today I felt the gripping power of my anger. I kept being imprisoned by violent, hostile feelings toward people who had not done for me what they had promised . . . my rage revealed the degree to which I still belong to this world and its promises and rewards."[17] I have had to say to God, "I am really mad, dangerously angry, almost out of control. Please help me!"

The great fourth-century preacher Gregory of Nazianzus spoke to God about his depression. "The breath of life, O Lord seems spent. My body is tense, my mind filled with anxiety, Yet I have no zest, no energy. . . . Dark thoughts constantly invade my head, And I have no power to resist them. . . . Lord, raise up my soul, revive my body."[18] I understand. After wrestling with reality, one day I had to pray, "I am depressed. I am tired. I am tired of being depressed. . . . My head is bent. My back aches. My chest is pushed down. . . . My feet feel like weights that make me shuffle rather than walk. My spirit sags. . . . I don't like this, God."[19]

Hildegard of Bingen confided in God about a problem of a different nature, a character trait as difficult as it is common. "How rigid and inflexible I am! I can overcome my own stubbornness only with the greatest difficulty. . . . But I cannot do it without you."[20]

Speaking to God about ourselves with such honesty constitutes far more than an act of "dumping on God." We are talking to our Lover. Honest communion between lovers carries within it inestimable value regardless of its content. One of George Matheson's prayers epitomizes the kind of honesty which God desires, as well as captures the significance of such honest sharing for the pray-er: "O my Father, I have moments of deep unrest—moments when I know not what to ask by reason of the very excess of my wants. I have in these hours no words for Thee, no conscious prayers for Thee. My cry seems purely worldly; I want only the wings of a dove that I may flee away. *Yet all the time Thou hast accepted my unrest as a prayer*" (italics mine).[21]

Expansive Love

As we open ourselves more and more to God's love, we are prompted toward greater, more comprehensive concern for other people. Love inspired by God refuses to tolerate prejudices and allow artificial boundaries. Lovers of God care for all of God's creation and creatures. Again, the New Testament writer named John places the matter in a proper perspective—this time bluntly: "If anyone says, 'I love God,' and hates his brother, he is a liar; for he who does not love his brother whom he has seen, cannot love God whom he has not seen" (1 John 4:20, RSV).

Lovers know how to talk lovingly about other people as well as themselves. This form of prayer requires complete honesty—even if it involves a confession of lovelessness towards other people.

While serving as Dean of Trinity College in Cambridge, Harry Williams prayed on one occasion, "O God, I am hellishly angry; I think so-and-so is a swine . . . here I am like this, feeling both bloody and bloody-minded, and I am going to stay here for ten minutes. You are most unlikely to give me anything. I know that. But I am going to stay for the ten minutes nonetheless."[22] *Oh, I could never say something like that to God* you may think. But think how much better it is to make such a statement to God than to anyone else. Besides, God wants a truthful admission of a problem, not a deceitful declaration that all is well.

Periodically, in a conversation with God, I try to assess the feelings which prompt my prayers for other people:

O God,

I want to be honest with others, but I don't want anyone to know me too well;

I want to be responsible, but I also want to keep some things to myself;

I want to be caring, but I know a few folks I have trouble even liking;

I want to be fair, but life is not fair;

I want to be Your faithful servant in this society, but You know how tough that is. Don't You?

Don't You, God?

When I find it difficult to pray for other people as I should, a portion of a prayer from Dominic Gaisford helps me: "Lord, I think what I really want from you in prayer is a huge pulsating heart to love you and other people, to live for you and others."[23] I want the same.

Thankfully, moments of clarity arrive when honesty about our life in society seems almost easy.

Our world is in trouble, God—big trouble. Anger runs rampant. Hatred dominates so many would-be communities. We try to justify murder in the name of national pride, political sovereignty, or responsible law enforcement—in the skies over Eastern Europe; across the borders of Syria, Israel, and Lebanon; and in the city streets of our land. Leaders meet events which could explode into war with political rhetoric filled with accusations. Even in a crisis, rabid nationalists refuse to shut down the machinery which spits out their propaganda. God, shock us into sanity. Call us again to the vocation of peace.

Social Vision

Honesty prompts lovers to share their positive visions as well as their questions and complaints related to social situations. The great Baptist minister and tireless social reformer Walter Rauschenbush prayed: "O God, grant us a vision of this city; . . . a city of justice, where none shall prey upon the other; a city of plenty, where vice and poverty shall cease to fester; . . . a city of peace, where order shall not rest on force, but on the love of all for each and all."[24]

The socially sensitive prayer of Rauschenbush brings to mind the vision of international peace so integral to the prophetic tradition in the Old Testament: "And they shall beat their swords into plowshares, and their spears into pruning hooks; nation shall not lift up sword against nation, neither shall they learn war any more" (Micah 4:3)

On a much less grandiose scale, I have spoken to God about scenes in society which lodged in my mind, challenged my conscience, and raised questions regarding the best way to respond to them.

O God,

Early this morning I saw a man sleeping on the steps of the courthouse protected from the chill of the wind only by a frost-covered newspaper.

Later I watched a group of stylishly clad investors lounging in leather chairs while studying ticker tape data spit out by computers on Wall Street.

At noon, as I walked to my parked car after enjoying a buffet luncheon at a fine downtown restaurant, I watched an elderly woman rummage through a garbage container until she happily discovered a partial loaf of stale bread and hurriedly lifted a piece of it into her mouth.

Something is wrong—God; badly wrong! I know it. But for the life of me, I don't know what to do about it. I don't even know where to start.

You have sensitized me to radical discrepancies in lifestyles which represent major injustices in our community. Now please, God, show me strategies for establishing equity and fill me with the courage to work on what I know is right.

Speaking the Truth in Love

Authentic personal prayer qualifies as a model response to the apostle Paul's admonition to speak the truth in love. Truth is to a love affair what blood is to a living body.

Lovers rightly view honesty as a non-negotiable in their relationship.

God expects honesty from us. Our love for God demands that we speak honestly to God. A dishonest statement cannot function as a prayer. Communion between lovers requires speaking the truth with love.

๛

CHAPTER SEVEN

I do not think one can pray in generalities
if prayer represents our deepest concerns.

E. Glenn Hinson, *A Serious Call to a Contemplative Lifestyle*

PRAYING SPECIFICALLY

Love affairs thrive on specifics. In the first place, a love affair involves specific people—a covenant between not just any lovers, but two particular lovers. That is not all, though. These lovers face unique situations, challenges, and problems. They find special meaning in specific experiences, words, and ideas.

Love between two lovers grows (or weakens) as a result of the way they handle the specifics of their relationship—whether or not they talk together about the joys, difficulties, sources of pleasure, and reasons for pain in their shared life. Each lover wants the other to detail activities ("Tell me about your day—tell me everything."), feelings ("I want to know how you really feel about what's going on."), problems ("What is bothering you?"), and needs ("Please let me know how I can best show you how much I love you."). Regular conversations about specific matters nurture communion between lovers.

Lovers value words, especially each other's words. A predictable conversation periodically occurs between long-time lovers. "Tell me that you still love me," one of them says to the other. "Why, you know I love you," comes the incensed response. "Yes, I'm sure you do, but I still like to be told. When we first met, you used to tell me all the things you liked about me. I need for you to do that again." There are no substitutes for words which convey the specifics of two people's love for each other.

God appreciates specifics. God chose to reveal the divine nature by acting in specific times and places, not by propagating a series of abstract ideas, theories, or generalizations. God declared the value of freedom not through general affirmations of liberty but by historical actions—delivering a particular group of slaves from captivity in Egypt and leading them home. God defined the nature of faith by calling Abraham, challenging Noah, and surprising Sarah—specific people. God commended love and mercy by taking on flesh in a specific person, Jesus of Nazareth.

Jesus revealed God in very specific ways. God spelled out God's mission in detail: "to proclaim release to the captives and recovery of sight to the blind, to let the oppressed go free" (Luke 4:18). Then God focused God's compassion on specific individuals—a man with a withered hand, a lady with a hemorrhage, hungry people, crazed people, and scores of others. When God's incarnate love faced its greatest challenge, rather than responding with a general affirmation of redemption and a vague endorsement of the value of sacrifice, Jesus submitted to an innocent death. God's sacrificial death caused even a pagan to say, "Truly this man was God's Son!" (Mark 15:39).

Like any other lover, the Divine Lover enjoys communion laced with specifics. The more we grow in our love for God, the more our prayers embrace the details of our days and the specifics of our interests.

I remember some of the bedtime prayers of my childhood. More than once, laying my head on a pillow, I quickly muttered something like, "God, You know all my sins, all my needs, and all my blessings. I'm sorry and I'm thankful. Please let that be enough for now. You know also all the people who need help. Please help them. Amen." My spiritual responsibility before sleeping was to pray, and these catch-all statements seemed to me more than adequate.

What a difference it makes to view God as a partner in a love affair. Prayers to God remain a responsibility, but a most happy one. The goal of a pray-er shifts from getting a prayer said out of obligation to strengthening our love affair by communing with God about every facet of life.

When we are honest with God, all the moods which surface in a love affair find expression in our prayers—joy, sadness, concern, anger, appreciation, and more. Likewise, our prayers contain a variety of concerns—selfish and unselfish, physical and emotional, professional and spiritual. Regardless of the concerns or moods of our prayers, however, we please God most by praying in specifics—communicating the specifics of our interests, feelings, and attitudes.

Adoration

The renowned poet Elizabeth Barrett Browning provided an exceptionally fine model for prayers of adoration. Most people know the beginning of her often-quoted sonnet, "How do I love thee? Let me count the ways." By way of poetic verse, Mrs. Browning conveyed the specifics of her love for her lover: "I love thee to the depth and breadth and height/My soul can reach . . . I love thee with the breath/Smiles, tears, of all my life!"[1] Specifics! How much better and more convincingly the poet conveys her love than if she had simply said, "I love you."

How do we love God? Specifically? We know how much God loves us. Through scriptural words and historical acts, God has demonstrated a love for us like no other love we have ever known. In prayers of adoration, we respond to God by detailing the nature of our reciprocal love.

I hate to admit it, but for a long time, I did not understand the role of adoration in prayer. Thus, my prayers seldom moved away from personal interests. I thanked God for blessings received, asked God's forgiveness for sins committed, requested God's help for everything from studying for a test to getting a new bicycle. But it never occurred to me to speak in detail about my love for God.

"Basically we are not into adoring God," one of my prayers began. "We find ourselves uncomfortable when people say nice things to us. Speaking to anyone else in positive terms alone presents us with problems. But You are different. Adoration takes effort, but You are worthy of our best efforts." I was learning the value and importance of adoring God.

William Temple called adoration the most selfless emotion of which our nature is capable and thus a remedy for the selfishness which leads to sin.[2] Prayers of adoration lift our eyes from ourselves and our surroundings and focus them on God. We seek to speak specifically of our love for God, to detail the attributes of God which elicit our love, appreciation, and gratitude.

Honestly, many of us find such prayer difficult. Once we have declared our love for God, we don't know what else to say. That very situation confirms our need for this particular kind of communication with God.

Borrow the poet's question and apply it to God: "How do I love thee?" Then try to count the ways. Recently I did that. With a prayerful desire to express my love for God in specifics, I took a pen and a sheet of paper and began to write down what I love about the nature of God. Among the words that I scribbled as a prayer were these:

I love Your creativity—the way You can fill an ordinary day with momentous experiences;
Your ability to turn a bad situation into an occasion for growth;
Your mercy which transforms episodes of sin into encounters with salvation.
I love Your affinity for beauty.
I love Your sense of humor.
I love Your steadfast presence.
I love Your vulnerability.
I love Your comfort.
I love Your commitment to community.
I love Your favor for underdogs.
I love Your passion for ministry, for peace, and for revelation.
I love what You do and who You are.
I love You for being You, God!

Prayers of Adoration

A study of other people's prayers helped me discover a variety of ways to express my adoration. Anselm piled adoring metaphor on top of majestic metaphor as he began a prayer, "O God, Thou art Life, Wisdom, Truth, Bounty, and Blessedness, the Eternal, the only true Good! My God and my Lord."[3] Inspired by the words of Psalm 31, Daniel Berrigan prayed, "How great is your goodness Lord/poured out on the one who loves you. . . . Hands aloft, you encompass a holy tent, a refuge."[4] Hymn writer Walter Chalmers Smith used his poetic gifts in adoration of God:

"Immortal, invisible, God only wise . . . Most blessed, most glorious . . . Almighty, victorious . . . Thou rulest in might . . . 'Tis only the splendor of light hideth Thee!"[5]

Francis of Xavier spent an entire night repeating, "My God and my All."[6] God's words were few, but his prayer was profound and specific—very specific. How better could Francis have told the God he loved of the all-consuming greatness of his adoration for God?

Biblical Examples

Of course, the Bible contains a wealth of adoration material. The psalmist exults, "Bless the LORD, O my soul, and all that is within me, bless his holy name"(103:1). Similarly, the seraphs in Isaiah's prophetic vision call to one another, "Holy, holy, holy is the LORD of hosts; the whole earth is full of his glory" (6:3). There are few adoring statements that can match this exclamation from King David found in 1 Chronicles 29:10–12:

> Blessed are you, O Lord, the God of our ancestor Israel, forever and ever. Yours, O Lord, are the greatness, the power, the glory, the victory, and the majesty; for all that is in the heavens and on the earth is yours; yours is the kingdom, O Lord, and you are exalted as head above all. Riches and honor come from you, and you rule over all. In your hand are power and might; and it is in your hand to make great and to give strength to all.

When we have trouble forming thoughts, words, and phrases of our own with which to adore God, we can borrow from the rich language of adoration in the Scriptures.

After reflecting on the Twenty-third Psalm for several days, I realized that the shepherd image of God did for the psalmist exactly what the lover image of God does for me. Viewing God as a shepherd enabled the psalmist to understand better the nature of God as well as provided him with a more focused means of meditating on God and communing with God. Inspired by the work of this ancient hymnist, I wrote my own prayer-psalm to God. I share the result not as a model but as an example of Bible-based, personal adoration.

The Lord is my lover, my guardian, my strong protector, who ministers to my needs and saves me from enslavement to my desires.

The Lord my lover counsels me to rest, and when I refuse to heed that advice, assists in my recovery from burnout or a breakdown.

The Lord my lover shows me a better way to live in which walking by still waters is as important as completing a task on schedule.

The Lord my lover gives me a sense of fulfillment, peace, and well-being; the Lord is the only one who can do that.

The Lord my lover leads me into causes that are just, enables me to make morally responsible decisions, and guides me through ethical ambiguity for the glory of God.

Even when I fall, fail, sin; when my life bottoms out and everything seems dark and heavy,

My lover stays with me, forgives my sin, relieves my guilt, picks me up, gives me strength, illuminates my path, and gets me going again.

When I find myself in a tough place, when my emotions are on edge, when I am ready to panic,

I look over my shoulder and see goodness and mercy following me. I watch God's grace not allowing me to travel beyond its reach.

And I know—though I don't know much—I know God is with me; my lover will never forsake me. And I realize that to be with God and to have God with me is to be safe—at home—forever. Amen.

Confession

Other people's opinions of us do not matter to us nearly so much as does the opinion of the one we love. We naturally want to please our beloved, to be on our best behavior for our lover, to present the best possible picture of who we are to the one we love. No wonder, then, we shy away from confession. Who wants to say to their beloved, "I blew it," "I sinned," "I betrayed our love," "I'm not the person you want me to be or that I desire to be"?

Reading the confessional prayer of Israel's revered King David, we can sense the depth of remorse in his soul, envision the pained look of sorrow on his face, and hear the agony of truth-telling in his voice. "Have mercy on me, O God. . . . I know my transgressions, and my sin is ever before me. Against you, you only, have I sinned, and done what is evil in your sight" (Ps. 51:1–4).

"Confessing our sins is the toughest work of worship."[7] And it well may be the most difficult dimension of prayer. One time I said to God, "Confessing my sins is like asking to have a tooth extracted or surgery performed. Disobedience has caused pain. The hurt of my sin is almost unbearable. But, as far as I can see, laying my condition before you will only result in more of the same—more pain and hurt. Confessing my sins is like pouring alcohol on an open, throbbing wound. I flinch because I fear it will hurt more."

Confession of Specific Sins

A general statement of confession is hard enough. Confessing the specifics of our wrongdoing requires every bit of effort we can muster. But intimacy requires detailed confessions—lovers confessing specific failures, weaknesses, and sins to each other. Only in dealing with the details of our wrongdoing do we confront the severity of betrayal, the hilarity of grace, and the matchless wonder of our lover's forgiveness.

Imagine a confessional conversation between two people in love with each other. With eyes cast downward, one says to the other, "I am sorry for what I did yesterday." Seldom, if ever, will the other lover respond with, "Oh, that's all right; don't mention it." Most likely the listener will say, "Tell me about it. What happened?"

Real lovers care about everything that happens in each other's lives, even those acts which cause hurt. In fact, a lack of concern for wrongdoing indicates an extremely shallow affection.

"Tell me about it," the listening lover says. "That's not necessary," the confessor mumbles, "Let's just leave it at that. I did wrong. I wanted you to know it. I've told you. Now, I hope we can drop it."

"No!" comes the emphatic response. "We can't drop it. I love you. I want to know what happened. You owe me that kind of honesty. Level with me." Such a demand arises not out of inquisitiveness or an interest in voyeurism, but compassion. Lovers take each other's behavior very seriously. Abiding, comprehensive concern is one of the attributes of love.

A prayer from the sixteenth century demonstrates the kind of specifics in confession which meet God's expectations. "Forgive me my sins, O Lord, forgive me the sins of my youth and the sins of mine age, the sins of my soul, and the sins of my body, my secret and whispering sins, my presumptuous and my crying sins, the sins that I have done to please myself, and the sins that I have done to please others. Forgive me those sins which I know, and those sins which I know not."[8]

I am not good at confession. I have trouble detailing my sins even in silent prayer. It is not only a matter of fearing how others may see me but of dreading how I will see myself. However, in search of God's forgiveness, I confess my sins:

God, forgive my incompleteness: not growing in Christ, not expanding my knowledge of the Scriptures, not developing all my talents.

God, forgive my disinterest: a lack of concern for needs around me, apathy regarding the lostness of millions, blindness to hurts I could help heal.

God, forgive my dishonesty: taking the easy way rather than the right way, speaking in one manner while living in another, silencing truth to preserve tranquility, settling for less than what is best, loving tradition more than obeying your pioneering Spirit.

God, forgive my loudness: talking when I should be listening, proclaiming when I should be studying, busying myself with new tasks when I should be finding a quiet place to rest.

God, forgive my silence: feeling love and failing to whisper it, reeling with joy and not shouting hallelujah, knowing truth and forfeiting an opportunity to share it, sensing a need to share my faith and squelching the impulse.

God, please forgive me.

Confession Leads to Hope

Detailed confessions of wrongdoing to the Eternal Lover differ substantially from self-deprecation, a scourging of the spirit which breaks the will, and a depersonalizing form of groveling. God seeks honest admissions of guilt from us. Keep in mind, though, that the purposes of confession between lovers are forgiveness, reconciliation, and renewal. No lover wants to see his beloved engage in a form of confession which destroys her dignity or develops a negative, defeatist attitude that erases all confidence that life can be better.

The prayer of David which began with such self-pity moved toward a recognition of hope: "Purge me with hyssop, and I shall be clean; wash me, and I shall be whiter than snow. . . . Create in me a clean heart, O God, and put a new and right spirit within me. . . . Then I will teach transgressors your ways. . . . And my tongue will sing aloud of your deliverance" (Ps. 51:7–14)

Aelred of Rievaulx displayed a similarly hopeful attitude toward confession when, after speaking candidly to God about his sins, he said, "Look well at me, sweet Lord, look well. I place my hope in your compassion, God of mercy, for you will look at me either like a caring physician bent on healing, or as a kind teacher anxious to correct, or again like the fondest of fathers, to excuse and overlook."[9]

Our true nature is defined as much by our relationship with God the Lover as by our sins. When we confess weaknesses and failures to God, we sketch images of our actions but we do not paint a complete picture of our character. A realistic portrait of who we are must somehow reflect the impact of our Lover's love.

King David committed adultery. But the Bible lauds David as "a man after God's own heart" (Acts 13:22). Adultery describes a part of David's activity. "A man after God's own heart" defines David's identity. Simon Peter betrayed the Lord he loved, yet the church points to Peter as a faithful disciple, not as a traitor. The Beloved God demonstrates a marvelous ability to see good potential in a sinner while taking the evil of his sin seriously.

Lovers speak to each other of the specifics of their sins, not to damage their relationship but so that out of the honesty of detailed confessions they can build an even greater intimacy. Comments of affirmation, joy, and praise lose their luster if lovers cannot trust each other to speak honestly and specifically about their sins. The hurt of confessions exchanged between lovers serves as a womb from which a healthy hope for their relationship is born.

In exemplary fashion, Catherine of Genoa refused to allow the severity of her sin to destroy her hope of being used for divine service. Catherine prayed, "I've been abysmally wrong, and I grieve for that. . . . But my world is bright, for I am surrounded and embraced by limitless love. The past is over. I will go now where love leads me."[10]

Intercession

Sharing Our Needs

Lovers know no unshared interests. Whatever concerns one concerns the other as well—if not immediately, at least eventually. Often the best revelations of our nature and the truest insights into the health of our love develop in our discussions about other people rather than in conversations focused exclusively upon ourselves.

Once we discover love, we dare not attempt to hoard it for ourselves. We don't even want to. Lovers find great joy in working together to solve problems, promote issues, head off difficulties, and others in situations whereby they have a great interest. Sharing concerns with one another leads to addressing these concerns together.

Intercessory prayer is a form of communion between lovers which focuses on the needs of other people. Moving beyond an interest in ourselves alone, we speak to God about persons and situations which elicit compassion from us. The more specifically we speak about our concerns to God, the more fulfilling is intercessory communion with our Lover.

Praying for Specific Needs

J. P. Allen once made the splendid suggestion that as we pray to God we imagine God talking back to us.[11] Such an effort benefits prayers of intercession considerably by forcing us to speak in specifics. When we pray, "God bless all the missionaries," we may hear God responding with, "What kind of blessing do you have in mind? What are their needs? Name the missionaries you know." Or, when we ask God to lead our church, we may have to respond to questions from God, "What kind of leadership do you want? What are the major leadership issues in your congregation? Are you willing to become a leader?"

Generalizations are cheap. Blanket statements roll out of our heads (seldom out of our hearts) and across our lips almost effortlessly—"God bless everybody"; "God help all who hurt." But, as Kathleen Norris observes, "God is in the details."[12] Prayers for particular people in specific situations resonate with a depth of love that is missing when we pray for everybody everywhere.

In a moving intercessory prayer for Jewish people, Henri Nouwen detailed his concerns before God: "Give them peace and freedom after the many centuries of persecution and oppression; give them a safe home in Israel; . . . give their children the 'Shalom' in its full sense of physical, mental, and spiritual well-being." Nouwen continued, "I pray especially that you give to the Jews the generosity of heart to keep forgiving us Christians for the cruelties and atrocities to which we have subjected them."[13]

Envisioning specific individuals with particular needs helps me in developing prayers of intercession. Though I will not include names here, in the course of a week I usually pray for: that family driving to the funeral home to work out burial arrangements for their son killed in an accident; the woman who screamed at me in anger—hurt because her husband is leaving her; the young man who learned today that he was not accepted to graduate school; the man who was terminated after his employer of thirty years became the victim of a hostile takeover; a teenager studying for her driver's license exam; the bearded man who walks the streets looking for food in garbage cans; friends who are attempting to start a new church in the face of heavy criticism; a woman struggling to defeat a temptation laced with the potential for serious damage.

Thanksgiving

Expressing thanks to one another becomes a kind of verbal dance of delight for lovers. Each word of thankfulness inspires their spirits to frolic in happiness. You can hardly tell who enjoys thanksgiving most: the one receiving it or the one offering it. Statements of gratitude grandly enrich the lives of both the lover and the loved.

Gerald Manley Hopkins captured the joy of thanksgiving as he spoke to God about the wonders of creation in poetic verse:

> *Glory be to God for dappled things—*
> *For skies of couple-colour as a brinded cow;*
> *For rose-moles all in stipple upon trout that swim;*
> *Fresh-firecoal chestnut-falls; finches' wings; Landscape plotted*
> *and pieced—fold, fallow, and plough.*[14]

A simple thank-you serves as a proper response to an act of kindness, an encouraging word, or a supportive spirit—as does "I appreciate it." But neither of these general comments means as much as a specific declaration of thankfulness—"Thank you for the beautifully written letter. I appreciate what you said and your willingness to use some of your valuable time to say it just right." Detailing reasons for our gratitude communicates a sensitivity, an awareness, and a degree of appreciation not conveyed by a blanket statement of thanks. Specific expressions of thankfulness nurture the generosity of love and strengthen the bond between lovers.

Some of my most meaningful prayers of thanksgiving focus on the people whom God has introduced into my life.

> God, I am thankful for the people to whom I can relate in all situations. I am grateful for all of them—for those called "family" who provide community, for those called "leaders" who give guidance, for those called "enemies" who help me see my faults, for those called "colleagues" who share responsibilities, for those called "scholars" who teach important lessons, for those called "helpers" who enable us to be of help, for those called "comforters" who dry my tears, unafraid of my weeping.

Usually I fill each category with a number of specific proper names.

I cannot come close to reproducing the poetic beauty of Gerald Manley Hopkins in my thanksgiving to God. But I can be equally specific about experiences for which I am grateful.

> Thank You, thank You, thank You, generous God!
> You have injected life with joy, thus we know laughter.
> You have dabbed creation with color, thus we enjoy beauty.
> You have whistled a divine tune into the rhythm of life, thus we hear music.
> You have filled our minds with questions, thus we appreciate mystery.
> You have entered our hearts with compassion, thus we experience faith.
> Thank You, God, thank You. Thank You!

The text of an old gospel song offers wise counsel: "Count your many blessings, name them one by one; count your many blessings see what God has done."[15] Heed that counsel—begin enumerating your specific blessings—and before you know it, you will be engaged in giving thanks to God.

Periodically, I find great joy in thanking God for gifts which do not regularly receive attention in my prayers.

> Generous God of love, today I am especially grateful for family reunions, get-togethers with old friends, introductions to new acquaintances; for picnics, popcorn, and caramel-covered apples; for squawking seagulls at the beach and soaring eagles in the mountains; for a field of bluebonnets in the spring and a grove of trees that looks like a bouquet of flowers in their autumn splendor.
>
> God, I know these blessings differ substantially from the gift of Your Spirit, the testimony of the Bible, and the power of Your redemption.
>
> But I am sincerely thankful for all Your gifts— blessings every one, blessings large and small.

Frankly, some people have trouble with this kind of prayer. A long-term preoccupation with reciting needs and making requests to God in prayer has silenced their litanies of joy and blinded them to experiences which should prompt words of appreciation. They seem to view God more as a heavenly bellhop than as their Lover. Though most thoughtful persons would never allow this attitude to prevail in conversations with an individual they love, they allow it to persist in relation to God.

More often than not, a careful look at a situation gives us as many reasons to thank God as to request something more from God.

> Loving God:
>
> To be run ragged all week and now to know both stillness and quietness; to be confused by contradictory advice and now to hear the consistent certainty of Your Word; to be plagued by guilt and hounded by temptation and now to know forgiveness and the strength of resistance; to be depressed and despondent and now to know the inspiration and exhilaration of Christian hope; is to be the blessed recipient of Your grace and kindness. Thank You God. Thank You so much.

Naming specific reasons for gratitude usually comes easily, but not always. Sometimes we are hurt, and hurt deeply. Though we may come through the experience stronger and more mature, nevertheless, we feel the pain. Giving thanks for such an experience is tough. We can't recall the good without remembering the bad. Expressing gratitude to God for such an experience, though, represents the highest form of thanksgiving and mature love. The greater our ability to thank God for the trials as well as the triumphs of life, the richer will be our love affair with God.

A man told me of his gratitude to God for time in prison. While incarcerated, he believed in Christ and was converted. I heard a married couple express thanks to God for a stressful period in which their marriage almost ended. Because of betrayals, arguments, and hurt, the couple faced long-standing problems, sought help, and moved toward a new and healthier level of love for each other. After complaining about his special difficulty and asking God to remove it from his life, the apostle Paul came to understand the "thorn in his flesh" as an opportunity for experiencing God's marvelous grace. How often an encounter with difficulty brings forth growth! The transformation inspires thanksgiving even as it points to the power of God to whom unending gratitude is in order.

Love in Details

God's people value specifics—specific revelation; specific persons, places, and times; a specific message; a focused love; a particular grace; a unique hope; a certain kind of faith. As the author of 1 John began to write a declaration of "the word of life," he emphasized the priority of "what we have heard, what we have seen with our eyes, what we have looked at and touched with our hands" (1:1)—the specific revelation of the One God in the Incarnation of Christ.

Speaking to God in specifics reflects the kind of loving communication which God wills for us and merits from us. The Divine Lover wants us to share the details of our thoughts, feelings, and needs related to the love affair. Whether at the height of ecstasy or in a pit of despair, God desires to know the particulars of our lives.

When we pray to God specifically, we pray lovingly; our prayers are saved from the boredom of platitudes or, worse still, from death by generalizations. Lovers delight in sharing with one another all the details of life.

᙮

CHAPTER EIGHT

Obedience is not as burdensome as it seems at first blush.
We are doing nothing more than falling head over heels in
love with the everlasting Lover of our souls.

Richard Foster, *Prayer: Finding the Heart's True Home*

PRAYING OBEDIENTLY

What great joy—often near ecstasy—lovers derive from pleasing one another. "Your wish is my command," a man whispers to his beloved, "I'll climb any mountain or swim any ocean just to see you smile." Lovers find tremendous fulfillment in meeting each other's needs, but even more in carrying out each other's wishes and exceeding each other's expectations.

Not surprisingly, then, the mutual desires so common in a love affair lead to actions which look completely ridiculous to detached observers.

Actually, loving God, obeying God, and praying to God can be separated only for purposes of discussion. Each is a melody integrally intertwined with the other two in the symphony of our faith. If we love God, we obey God. We obey God because we love God. As the author of 1 John explained, we demonstrate the love of God in our lives by obeying God's word (2:5). Likewise, if we obey God, we pray to God. A desire to obey our Lover, to please

God, births our prayers to God. Subsequently, in obeying God and praying to God, our love for God grows.

Obedient prayers to God meet God's expectations for pray-ers. Through the message of the Bible generally and in the teachings of Jesus particularly, God issued calls for particular types of communion. A love affair with God may involve much more than obedient responses to God's specific requests, but never less.

Pray to God

Call God a jealous lover if you will, but God seeks to be the sole recipient of our prayers. Actually, what looks like jealousy is God's propensity to demand of us what is best for us.

Jesus taught us how to pray. God's model prayer helps us immensely. The Holy Spirit assists in prayer, providing us with strength to emulate the model of Jesus and supplying us with words (or at least sighs and groans) for communion when, on our own, we come up empty.

Jeremiah wrote of God's will regarding prayer, "You will call upon me and come and pray to me, and I will hear you. You will seek me and find me; when you seek me with all your heart, I will be found by you, says the LORD" (29:12–14, RSV). Then, as a faithful prophet of God, Jeremiah instructed his followers to "pray to the LORD your God" (42:2).

Every time Jesus offered a prayer or taught others to pray, God first acknowledged God as the One to whom God's prayers were offered: "Our Father who art in heaven" (Matt. 6:9), "My Father" (Matt. 26:39, 42), "Abba, Father" (Mark 14:36). Followers of Jesus, such as Paul, did likewise: "I thank my God" (Phil. 1:3), "I bow my knees before the Father" (Eph. 3:14), "We always thank God" (Col. 1:3).

Praying to God differs dramatically from casting a wish into the wind. Prayer cannot be contained in clichéd categories such as "a shot in the dark," "a venture into the vast unknown," or "a shout to the heavens." Prayer grows out of a relationship between lovers. Obedient prayer consists of honest communion with God—an intimate, personal act (whether verbal or nonverbal) in which we present the entirety of our beings to the God who loves all of creation and every person in it.

Praise God

We give expression to the most fundamental aspect of our nature when we praise God. We were created to praise God.

Passage after passage in the Bible calls forth our praise for God. From the psalmist comes a redundant mandate in a variety of forms: "Praise the LORD!" (104:35), "You who fear the LORD, praise him!" (22:23), "Praise, O servants of the LORD; praise the name of the LORD" (113:1), "Let everything that breathes praise the LORD!" (150:6). The prophet Jeremiah calls forth songs and shouts of praise for God (31:7). Jesus inspired praise among people who greeted God (Luke 19:37). Paul demanded praise for God among Gentile believers (Rom. 15:11). The apocalyptic vision of Revelation includes a commission to praise: "Praise our God, all you his servants" (19:5). Each biblical summons to praise coincides with relentless tugs within our hearts.

God mandates praise, not as a self-serving, egotistical being, but as one who loves us and knows we function best as whole persons when we give praise to God. What we need to do and have to do coincides with what we want to do—praise God.

Most of the time praise comes easily. Many of my prayers of praise look and sound very much alike.

Praise be to You, O God!

The beauty of the earth proclaims the glory of Your creation. I praise You, O God.

The ministry of the church heralds the breadth of Your compassion and the power of Your redemption. I praise You, O God.

The faith of Christian disciples cries out about the wonders of Your grace. I praise You, O God.

I will continually praise You whether times are good or bad; whether health is sound or poor; whether life is full or empty.

I will praise You with my words, thoughts, and actions; with my lips, hands, and feet; with my hymns, prayers, and offerings.

Please accept my praise Lover God. I love You, adore You, worship You, and desire to serve You.

But praise is not always easy, not even between lovers. Situations develop in which praise seems buried in the depths of our souls and covered by a mountain of negative emotions. Neither internal feelings nor external conditions, however, nullify the command to praise God. Indeed, the highest form of personal praise develops when we praise God while struggling with difficulties and feeling unblessed, if not forgotten, by God.

When I have trouble offering praise to God, I ask for assistance: "God, help me, please. Enable me to find the resources with which to praise You in hospitals as well as in houses, in funeral homes as well as in nurseries, in failures as well as in successes, in mistakes as well as on missions."

Perspective is so important in maintaining the proper attitude for offering praise. Even when a specific situation makes praising God appear to be a problem, I find that a larger vision of God makes praise possible.

Lover God:

I have known bitterness, but I have tasted sweetness from You.

I have hidden my face in fear, but I have felt Your gift of courage in my heart.

I have been rocked by doubts only to have You strengthen my faith.

I have felt all alone, but You have sent a friend to me or provided a supportive fellowship.

I have grieved beside the grave of a family member, but I have also laughed at the cry of a newborn child.

I have worried over reports of conflict, but I have been cheered by promises of peace.

I have grown melancholy as autumn leaves fell, but I have sensed ecstasy as jonquils pushed their blooms through the soil silently trumpeting spring.

God, help me.

I want to praise You amid bitterness as in sweetness, in times of doubt as well as moments of faith, in solitude and society, in grief and happiness, in peace and amid conflict, and in every season of the year.

Right now, I am hurting, God. But I also am praising You as best I know how.

At our best, we praise God apart from demands or commandments. The impulse of our love is stronger and quicker than our obedience to written law. We praise God because of who God is—Creator, Redeemer, and Ultimate Lover—and because of who we are—redeemed creations of God in love with our Beloved Creator-Redeemer.

Pray for the Spread of the Gospel

Both Jesus and the apostle Paul requested prayers for the ministry of the gospel and for ministers of the gospel. Jesus instructed God's disciples to pray for enough messengers of the gospel to share the good news with all people ready to receive it (Matt. 9:37–38; Luke 10:2–3). Then, in a prayer of His own, Jesus asked God "to protect" heralds of the gospel (John 17:15).

Paul asked his brothers and sisters in Christ for their intercessory prayers of support for his work related to the gospel—that he might have many opportunities to share the good news of Christ as well as the ability to proclaim that news with clarity (Col. 4:3–4). In his own prayers, the apostle regularly pleaded for a broad-based acceptance of the gospel (Rom. 10:1) and frequently thanked people whom he knew had supported the spread of the gospel in their communion with God (2 Cor. 1:11).

Sometimes I do not know exactly how to speak to God about the gospel. When I seem at a loss for prayerful thoughts and phrases focused on creative strategies for personal witnessing, innovative approaches to ministry, and other forms of sharing the gospel, I often begin to speak with God about my gratitude for the gospel. "O God of Good News, thank You for those people of old who under the guidance of Your spirit wrote down the truths of the gospel; thank You for the preservation of this material in the Bible; thank You for scholars who translated the gospel into a language I understand; and thank You for the women and men who have helped me apply the gospel to my life."

Extended reflection on the importance of the gospel and thoughtful thanksgiving for the ministry of the gospel usually make me aware of the tremendous challenges involved in sharing the gospel. I pray:

God,

the challenge of the gospel is almost overwhelming . . .

to speak good news to people conditioned to hear bad news;

to act redemptively amid forces wielded vindictively;

to live peaceably in the face of threats of war;

to call people to wholeness when all they know is fragmentation;

to opt for service in a society preoccupied with success—God, the challenge is so big!

Keep ever before me the true nature of a gospel witness—to share the message of salvation, not just to speak;

to nurture faith and faithfulness, not just to enlist followers;

to show forth Christ, not just to garner support for a particular culture or point of view.

Once I begin to commune with God about the gospel, speaking to God about the spread of the gospel comes more easily. Though I did not know what to think or say at first, words and thoughts begin to flow freely. In communion with God, I discover God giving me the words I need to pray in an obedient, pleasing manner. Such a transaction happens between lovers all the time.

At this point, my prayer for the spread of the gospel becomes very personal: "God, please allow the gospel truths embedded in Scripture to become embodied in my life." Then, come a series of simple requests:

God, bless the gospel witness of my words.

Give me insights into when to speak, to whom, and how. God, enhance the gospel witness of my actions. Let me so live that the manner of my life attracts others to live similarly.

(A shudder runs through my soul as I mouth this last sentence.)

God, strengthen the gospel witness of my mind. Enable me through spirit and voice to display a devotion to truth unaccompanied by a fear of old questions and new insights in order that others may come to know Christ as Truth.

Pray for Other People

The more we love God, the more we will love other people. A vision of God which results in greater obedience to God

123

intensifies our concern for other people. As lovers in communion with God, we naturally speak with God about various individuals and groups of people within our global community.

Even ancient mystics who virtually withdrew from the world to concentrate on deepening their devotion did not fail to pray for other people. Augustine observed, "We love God and our neighbor from one and the same love."[1] Similarly, Teresa of Avila commented, "We cannot know whether or not we love God . . . but we can know whether we love our neighbor. And be certain that the more advanced you see you are in love for your neighbor the more advanced you will be in the love of God."[2]

A love affair with God inspires a compassionate interest in the people whom God loves—which means everybody. Little wonder, the author of 1 Timothy asserts, "I urge that supplications, prayers, intercessions, and thanksgivings be made for everyone" (2:1). Eager to obey that biblical admonition, John Wesley prayed, "Suffer me to exclude none, O Lord, from my charity, who are the objects of your mercy; but let me treat all my neighbors with that tender love which is due to your servants and to your children."[3]

Prayers on behalf of some people come easily. No one has to tell us to pray for family members, colleagues at work, persons in our church, and neighbors on our street. Talking to God on behalf of these individuals comes as naturally as breathing. Likewise, we typically pray for people bothered by an illness, thus almost thoughtlessly obeying the admonition of James 5:13. "But, what else would a caring person do?" you ask. Precisely—the question makes the point. Care leads to prayer.

Biblical instructions on prayer expand the extent of our care, broadening our compassion to include people we might otherwise exclude (unintentionally or intentionally). God mandates prayers which stretch the boundaries of our love. God commands us to love, which removes all restrictions governing the people for whom we pray.

Government Officials

Biblical writers viewed government officials as servants of God worthy of respect and needful of prayers from the people of God—all the officials (1 Tim. 2:1–2). Such a perspective on political leaders could be expected as long as ancient citizens believed their kings ascended to the throne as a result of the anointing of God. But, surprisingly, the same point of view continued even when evil sovereigns ruled the land. Admonitions to pray for the king persisted from the time of Ezra (6:10) through the days of the Roman peace which benefited Christians (Rom. 13:1–7) into periods when Christians suffered severe persecutions at the hands of civil rulers (1 Pet. 3:13–17).

Several years ago, I found myself not only opposed to the policies of a certain civic leader but also angered by the immoral and illegal tactics with which he ran his office. One day while I was complaining about the policies of this man to a friend, obviously sympathetic with my opinions, my friend startled me by asking, "Are you praying for this politician?" I quickly responded negatively and then incredulously asked, "Are you praying for him?" She explained that she was spending fifteen minutes a day in prayer for this official.

My friend represented the posture of a true lover of God. In a democracy, we have the luxury of deciding whom we will support with a vote. But as lovers of God we face the requirement of praying for all who participate in the political process.

Peter Marshall's prayers for national leaders point the way to meaningful communion with God about all who are a part of the political situation: "Save our leaders, O God, from themselves and from their friends—even as Thou has saved them from their enemies."[4] Whether praying for civil servants as a group, or for specific officials in particular positions of power, Marshall's prayers embraced certain common themes: "Let no personal ambition blind them to their opportunities. Help them to give battle to hypocrisy wherever they find it. Give them divine common sense and a selflessness that shall make them think of service and not of gain."[5]

Enemies

Just the thought of praying for our enemies cuts across the grain of our wills. Such prayers are not natural; they run counter to our strongest impulses. As Henri Nouwen rightly observes, to pray for a person means "to enter into a deep inner solidarity" with that individual "so that in and through us" the person "can be touched by the healing power of God's Spirit."[6] Who wants that for an enemy? Yet Jesus instructed us to love our enemies and to pray for those who persecute us (Matt. 5:43–44).

Nowhere does the necessity of love's discipline become more apparent than in prayers for enemies. Out of an abiding love for God and a sincere desire to obey God, we force ourselves to pray for our enemies. Subsequently, we may see as never before the power of prayer. While praying for our enemies, we start to understand and appreciate them as well as open ourselves to the possibility of a friendship with them.

I readily identify with a prayer from the highly respected South African writer Alan Paton: "Lord, teach me the meaning of your commandment to love our enemies, and help me to obey it. Make me an instrument of your love. . . . Teach me to hate division, and not to seek after it. But teach me also to stand up for those things that I believe to be right, no matter what the consequences may be."[7] Much in that same spirit, I have prayed, "Reconciling God: If I must have enemies, let me have them for good reasons. Even then, though, help me to relate to these enemies in a manner which can lead to us becoming friends."[8]

In a prayer requesting God to help him love his enemies, Anselm of Canterbury offered a powerful prayer on behalf of his enemies,

"If I ever ask for them anything
Which is outside your perfect rule of love,
Whether through weakness, ignorance or malice,
Good Lord, do not give it to them
And do not give it back to me."[9]

Make Requests

Lovers cannot be indifferent about anything of major concern to their beloveds. As our Lover, God demands (and invites) that we share our personal concerns in prayerful communion. Nothing of ultimate importance to God can be inconsequential for us, and vice versa.

After Saul of Tarsus became a Christian, he stayed in constant communion with God. A scan of the apostle's prayers preserved in the New Testament reveals the variety of subjects properly embraced in requests to God. Paul asked God for comfort (2 Cor. 1:3–4), peace (2 Thess. 3:16), harmony among Christians (Rom. 15:5), growth in grace (Rom. 15:13), and understanding (Phil. 1:9).

A review of other people's prayers sensitizes me to requests which I need to lay before God and inspires me to be more comprehensive in what I ask of God. Here is a sampling of prayer requests which comprise obedient communion with our Lover.

Forgiveness

Almost every time I speak to God, I end up asking for forgiveness. The closer my prayers draw me to God, the more uncomfortable I become with my failure to be the person God created me to be. So, over and over again I request God's forgiveness. My repetition of this request stems not from God's unwillingness to grant forgiveness but from my continuing need to experience it.

At times, I voice a simple request for forgiveness: "O God, before sleep closes my eyes at the end of this day, please forgive the wrongs which could rightly keep me awake all night." At other times, I speak to God in more detail: "Loving God, please forgive my sins of recent weeks—those which I committed in secret; those which I bragged about; those which harmed creation; those which hurt other people; those which tarnished the church; those which I failed to see as sin until now; those which I knew full well were wrong all along."

God's forgiveness is sure; we can count on it. But self-forgiveness is often problematic. Occasionally, I thank God for divine forgiveness and then make a different kind of request: "God, please help me forgive myself. Enable me to bathe myself with the same grace in which You have baptized me."

Jan Ruysbroeck understood the pain and the promise involved in requesting God's forgiveness: "To be wounded by love is the sweetest feeling and the sharpest pain which anyone may endure. To be wounded by love is to know for certain that one shall be healed."[10] George Fox expressed the same truth with these words, observing that the God "who shows a man his sin is the same that takes it away."[11]

Peace

Requests for peace may take the form of loud screams or inarticulate sighs. God hears, understands, and accepts both. "My soul feels like a battlefield, God!" I have prayed, "The apostle Paul had nothing on me. I don't do the good I want to do. I end up doing the evil I resolve not to do. A war between good and evil rages within me. Casualties mount—my sanity, my health, my faith. O God, please give me peace!"

A Christian concern for peace stretches around the globe as well as reaches into the heart and focuses on warring armies even as on hostile temptations. Through the ages, God's people have prayed for social reconciliation and international peace. The ancient patriarch Dionysius of Alexandria requested God to:

> "Make up
> The dissensions which divide us
> From each other,
> And bring us back
> Into the unity of love,
> Which to thy divine nature
> May bear some likeness."[12]

In much the same spirit, though separated from Dionysius by nearly nineteen centuries, noted preacher Theodore Parker Ferris asked God to "give to the nations of the world the imagination and the will to reject once and for all war and the weapons of war."[13]

Understanding

Life baffles me at times. Some experiences leave me feeling like I just stepped off one of those jerky, whirling rides at a carnival. To be perfectly honest, though I want God's help, I don't even know how to pray about my situation. All I can do is request understanding.

> God, I'm really confused. I want Your help. I need Your help. But, I don't know how best to ask for it.

In the midst of this awful summer heat, should I ask for relief through cooling rains or for protection for the people most ill effected?

In my sickness, should I request healing or endurance?

Facing my anxieties, should I ask for major alterations or common patience?

Struggling with day-to-day difficulties, ought I to be requesting miracles or more adeptness in coping?

God, help me sort through my confusion. God, please grant me understanding.

Frequently, before studying a passage in the Bible, I ask God to help me understand the truth in front of me and its importance for my life. A prayer for enlightenment from John Hunter captures the sentiments which I convey to God: "Blessed Lord, who hast caused all sacred Scriptures to be written for our learning . . . we desire of Thee the gifts of insight and wisdom, or patience and charity, so to read the letter of things written in olden times, that Thy Holy Spirit of truth may ever live in us; and that we may so meditate on the story of things temporal, as ever to worship Thee the Living and Eternal God."[14]

Likewise, I often make requests of God based upon the thoughts and feelings engendered by the study of a passage of Scripture. The following prayer is not uncommon:

I have heard Your Word again, God.

The text is familiar to me. But, honestly, it has a strange ring about it. I sense discontinuity between Your will and my ways. At moments the chasm which seems to separate Your Word and our world tempts me toward discouragement.

I imagine that giving up on trying would relieve the tension between Your expectations and our actions.

O God, grant me patience—courageous patience—that I may continue to wait before Your Word, to hear Your truths, and to implement Your will in my life.

Instill in me truths from texts which I did not study today—Your confidence in us, Your grace to us, and Your presence with us—that I may know the power and assurance which enable me to translate the words of a Scripture passage into activities which fill my days.

Deliverance

Requests for deliverance dot the text of the Bible. Joshua asked God to deliver him from death (2:13), Job requested deliverance from his enemies (6:23), the psalmist prayed for deliverance from the ravages of illness (6:4) and wicked people (17:13), and, in God's model prayer, Jesus taught everyone to ask God for deliverance from evil (Matt. 6:13).

Not all requests for deliverance focus on burdens imposed by physical conditions. A woman pleads for God's assistance as she attempts to stop a bad habit. An offended man asks God to deliver him from enslavement to a hatred which is slowly eating away at his spirit. Friends pray for God to rescue them from a spiritual sink-hole of prejudice.

Wanting to see God's glory and fearful of insensitivity, the great Italian artist Michelangelo prayed,

"Dear Lord . . .
raise Me from the misery of this blind woe,
Your spirit alone can save me: let it flow
Through will and sense, redeeming what is base."[15]

Similarly, fighting servitude to fatigue, the great German composer Ludwig van Beethoven asked God to raise his spirit "from these weary depths, that ravished by your Art, it may strive upwards with tempestuous fire."[16]

Reading about God's involvements in history drives us to conclude that our grand Lover is a great deliverer.

Meaningful reflection on that dimension of God's identity almost certainly gives rise to requests for acts of divine deliverance in our lives.

Great God of Love and Deliverance:

I stand in awe of Your ability to get people out of tough situations.

I marvel at Your deliverance of Israel from slavery in Egypt, deliverance of Daniel from the lion's den, deliverance of Shadrach, Meshach, and Abednego from the fiery furnace, deliverance of Mary, Joseph, and Jesus from the horrors of King Herod's jealous anger, and deliverance of Paul from the crazed crowd at Ephesus.

God, I thank You for the promise conveyed through all these merciful acts of deliverance.

O God, deliver me!

Deliver me from thoughts which erode my spirit, from intentions which compromise Your will, from doubts which destroy faith, from gossip which harms all involved in it, from dishonesty in beliefs, words, and behavior, from failures of courage to live by my convictions.

Deliver me, God!

Physical Conditions

Assured of God's concern about our total well-being, we please God when our prayers convey requests related to our physical condition. Paul the apostle modeled obedient, loving prayer when he requested God to remove his "thorn in the flesh" and thus spare him the pain it caused (2 Cor. 12:7–9).

Many of my prayers of request related to troublesome physical conditions are short and to the point. But I know my Lover understands them; God understands me. "I need rest, God. I'm bone tired. Please help me rest." "O God, I am hurting. Whether the pain is physical or emotional or both, I'm not sure. Please God, either remove the hurt or help me cope with it better." "I am tired of not feeling good. Could You please help me, God? I want to be well again."

Church

Immediately prior to God's death, Jesus prayed at length for the church. Interceding with God on behalf of members of the fellowship of faith, Jesus asked God to "protect them from the evil one," to "sanctify them in the truth," and to make them "one, as we are one, I in them and you in me" (John 17:15, 17: 22–23).

Likewise, the apostle Paul prayed regularly for the church. In an extended prayer for the Christian congregation at Ephesus, Paul requested God to enlighten the members that they might know "the hope" to which God had called them and "the riches of his glorious inheritance among the saints, and what is the immeasurable greatness of his power for us who believe" (Eph. 1:18–19). Later, he prayed again for the same congregation, that God "according to the riches of his glory . . . may grant that you may be strengthened. . . with power through his Spirit . . . and that Christ may dwell in your hearts through faith, as you are being rooted and grounded in love . . . that you may have the power to comprehend, with all the saints, what is the breadth and length and height and depth, and to know the love of Christ that surpasses knowledge, so that you may be filled with all the fullness of God" (Eph. 3:16–19).

My requests to God related to the church tend to be extremely practical in nature. "God, please strengthen our fellowship, give us vision, make us bold, challenge us, nurture our faithfulness, bless our gifts, and direct our ministries." Every time I pray for the church, I also have to say to God, "I realize that to pray for the church is to pray for myself as well as other people. What I have asked

You to do in and with others, O God, I also ask You to do within me."

Make a Commitment

Lovers recognize the need for making a commitment to each other. Each longs to hear the other say, "I am committed to you for life." Commitment provides the stability, trust, and communion so necessary for the development of intimacy.

From the Old Testament's admonition, "Commit your work to the LORD" (Prov. 16:3) to the Gospels' accounts of Jesus' call to discipleship, "Follow me" (Matt. 16:24; Mark 8:34; Luke 9:23), God draws us toward a committed relationship. God chooses us as partners in a love affair marked by covenantal devotion and unconditional commitment. Because commitment pledges us to respond obediently to all of God's other loving directions, no other prayer exceeds a prayer of commitment in importance. Responding to God's love with a commitment nurtured by love constitutes the epitome of obedience to God.

A twelfth-century disciple named Aelred of Rievaulx captured the elements of intimacy and resolve in a prayer of commitment: "Dear Lord Jesus, the fragrance of your love draws me towards you, like the perfume of the beloved attracts her lover. I shall follow you. . . . I will not desert you when you walk to Calvary. I shall stay beside you, and follow your body when it is taken to the tomb. Let my flesh be buried with you. . . . I no longer wish to live for myself, but to rise with you into the fullness of your love."[17]

The consequences of commitment, not all of which are pleasant, give rise to additional prayers of commitment or recommitment. Ignatius of Loyola understood both the cost and the importance of commitment as he prayed, "Teach us, good Lord, to serve you as you deserve: To give and not to count the cost; To fight and not to heed the wounds; To toil and not to seek for rest; To labor and not to ask for any reward Save that of knowing that we do your will."[18]

Not all my prayers of commitment to God soar to such heights. More than once I have spoken about commitment to God with embarrassing candor:

Good and loving God:
Sometimes, like now, I would like to renegotiate this matter of commitment. It seems so full and final.

Would You settle for one day a week or one talent out of several or a percentage of our money rather than all of it?

Would You settle for less than everything in life?
. . . . Of course not.

You gave everything. Everything!
Here is my life, O God.

Even when my commitment is weakest, I aspire to a greater, stronger commitment. Teresa of Avila spoke to God in a mood and manner which I would like to emulate: "I am yours, you made me. I am yours, you called me. I am yours, you saved me. I am yours, you loved me. I will never leave your presence."[19] During moments in which I can't honestly offer that prayer to God as my own, I pray for a quick arrival of the time when I can.

I want my life to be as completely committed to God as the life which Dwight L. Moody described in one of his prayers of commitment: "Use me, my Savior, for whatever purpose and whatever way you may require. . . . Take my heart for your abode; my mouth to spread abroad the glory of your name; my love and all my powers for the advancement of your believing people; and never allow the steadfastness and confidence of my faith to abate."[20] Such commitment necessitates the kind of self-abandonment conveyed in a prayer by Charles de Foucauld: "Father, I abandon myself into your hands; do with me what you will. . . . I am ready for all, I accept all. Let only your will be done in me. . . . I wish no more than this, O Lord."[21]

Love and Obedience

In our relationship with God, obedience may precede love. Sometimes we respond positively to God's guidance more out of discipline than desire. But consistent obedience to God leads inexorably to love. And faithful love for God always results in obedience.

Relating to God with loving obedience often draws charges of foolishness from skeptical onlookers. Critics label as "clownish" endeavors such as praying for enemies, seeking forgiveness, asking for God's assistance in a political arena, working to ease a massive problem like hunger, and remaining faithful to a church. So be it. Invariably lovers look like fools to those not in love, and servants seem like clowns to seekers of power and success.[22]

Our obedient prayers to God deepen our love for God and enrich the communion which is the substance of our love affair with God.

❧

CHAPTER NINE

Eternal Father of my soul,
let my first thought today be of thee,
let my first impulse be to worship thee,
let my first speech be thy name,
let my first action be to kneel before thee in prayer.

John Baillie, *A Diary of Private Prayer*

PRAYING PERSISTENTLY

Lovers thrive on keeping in touch. No one has to tell them to make contact with each other. They live for such experiences. Lovers want to talk to each other as many times a day as possible. The communion they share gives meaning and joy to their lives. Each finds the greatest amount of personal fulfillment when communion with the other is most constant.

A love affair with God evokes persistent prayer. Once we know the wonder and power of communion with God, we don't ever want to be out of touch with God. How we feel, how busy we are, what all remains to be done, and how easy or difficult reaching out to God may be do not matter. Nothing receives a higher priority among lovers of God than communion with God.

Jesus commended persistence in prayer; He spoke of people's "need to pray always" (Luke 18:1). The repetitive instructions of Jesus—"ask . . . search . . . knock" (Matt. 7:7)—represent neither a magic formula which pray-ers can use to guarantee getting what they request nor the picture of an obstinate God who has to be cajoled into listening to the words of those who pray. Jesus' endorsement of aggressiveness in prayer arose out of God's recognition of the sheer joy of prayer.[1] This same emphasis upon repetitive prayer runs through at least two of the parables of Jesus (Luke 11:5–8; 18:1–8). Clearly, Jesus called for persistence in prayer because He knew the happy fulfillment of unbroken communion with God and desired for all God's followers to know the same.

Paul reflected the teachings of Jesus in his message and ministry. Writing to Christians in Thessalonica, the apostle shared an admonition which stretches across the centuries and addresses us as well: "pray constantly" (1 Thess. 5:17, RSV).

"Wait just a minute," someone protests, "I don't do anything constantly except breathe." Exactly—that is the point. Prayer is as essential to living as breathing. In a love affair with God, communion with God fills every moment.

Memorable Models

Amid the beautiful rolling terrain which surrounds Bardstown, Kentucky, sets the aging Abbey of Gethsemani. Behind the walls of this unimpressive structure resides a community of Trappist Monks. For many years, Gethsemani was home for Thomas Merton. Every man who enters the Trappist Order takes vows of poverty, work, and silence—strict disciplines intended to encourage a life of prayer.

I made my first visit to Gethsemani with a somewhat skeptical, if not outright critical, attitude toward this monastic order. I surmised that these mystical, hooded figures must be running from the world, escaping life—hardly a theologically justifiable action in a world with so many needs, in my opinion. Their lifestyle struck me as strange: prayers beginning at 2:00 A.M.; corporate worship two or three times a day; hard work in the fields; silent meditations during meals; and more prayers—indeed persistent, constant prayer. After spending a day in this community, however, I changed my mind about the people living there.

The abbot at Gethsemani grants chosen monks permission to break their vow of silence so they can serve as hosts to visitors to the monastery. Conversing with our assigned host for the day, a member of my group asked, "How do you justify living so completely apart from the world?" The defensiveness from the monk which I anticipated did not appear. Instead, after observing how God calls people to many different tasks, our host explained that residents of Gethsemani had experienced a divine summons to a life of prayer. God spoke of the monks' respect for people who function obediently in all the various callings from God. Then he said, "Our ministry is prayer. We pray for the world. We pray for the success of the gospel in the world. We pray for people in all areas of life. We view our ministry of prayer to be as important as other functions in life, more important than most."

Never before had I heard such a moving statement about the importance of constant prayer. The lifestyle of the speaker strengthened the impact of his words. This man had placed his life where his conviction pointed. My first visit to Gethsemani changed me. Since that day, I have viewed prayer as a profoundly important act of communion with God, which the people of God should engage in persistently.

Of course, most people don't live in a monastery. Thankfully, persistence in prayer can occur independently of where we live.

Years after my visit to the Gethsemani monastery, I made a pastoral call on an elderly lady confined to her house by a serious illness. This woman told me how much she missed attending her church. However, the woman's comments flowed unburdened by self-pity. She happily described how she envisioned prayer as the ministry to which she was called at this time in her life. Her words stuck in my mind, "Someone has to do the praying."

Once again, an unforgettable image seared truth into my conscience about the importance of persistent prayer. Though both of the models so significant to me involved people confined to one place, I knew that constant communion with God did not require a person to remain in the same spot forever.

Several years ago, while Jimmy Carter campaigned for the presidency of the United States, he became the butt of innumerable jokes about his spiritual life. Responding to a reporter's question about his prayer life, candidate Carter explained that he prayed all the time. He spoke of praying while waiting for a traffic light to change, while walking, and during all kinds of other engagements. Many members of the media judged Carter's comments to be hilarious, if not ridiculous. Scores of people read his comments about prayer and laughed. But Jimmy Carter's revelation about his personal prayer life provided an excellent insight into the meaning of God's expectation of all of us—that we pray persistently.

Times of Prayer

Prayer is both timely and timeless. Certain situations evoke prayer more readily than others. Prayer seems more appropriate on some occasions than on others. However, prayers never have to be delayed until a particular time or circumstance. Like communion between lovers, prayer remains always appropriate—and essential.

Late one evening I stood in a hospital chapel trying to comfort a man whose wife was dying. The disturbed husband asked if I would voice a prayer for his spouse, explaining, "I believe in prayer. But I don't pray much, if at all. I guess now that I need to pray, I really don't know how." This fellow's words brought to mind the necessity of constancy in prayer and raised questions in my mind about how meaningful communion with God can best be maintained.

Feelings Fail as Guides

A lot of people declare that they pray when they feel like it or really want to. At other times, they don't bother themselves about the need to pray. If we take that approach to prayer—speaking with God only when we feel just right or find ourselves troubled by a major challenge—we probably fall woefully short of persistence in our prayers.

Communion between lovers does not depend upon feelings. Lovers persist in their efforts to communicate with each other in good times and bad, during sickness as well as health, when failure hits as well as when success arrives. As a matter of fact, two lovers' ability to commune with each other when they don't especially feel like it impacts their capacity to converse with each other in times of great stress or extreme joy.

We can no more discard praying because we are not in the mood than we can stop breathing because we don't feel like making the effort. Regular communication with God is a basic necessity in the lives of all who love God—a dimension of our existence no more optional than eating, drinking, and sleeping.

Remember, though, we don't have to fake it with God. When we feel like we have fallen into a deep pit, we have no obligation to speak to God as if we had just scaled a great mountain. We are talking to our Lover. Lovers prize honesty. In difficult times, our prayers may consist of relating to God why we don't feel like praying.

During one particularly difficult time in my life, I prayed:

I don't feel like praying, God, because I don't know what to say. But I know I need to pray. And I want to.

God, You once said that sometimes the Spirit intercedes for us to make known our thoughts, feelings, and sensations which we cannot verbalize.

That promise gives me great comfort because, in moments like this one, I neither know what to say in prayer nor what to think about prayer.

I feel inexpressible joy, God. I know the reasons why I feel it, but I don't know how to tell You about it.

I have indefinable needs, God. I know what they are, but I don't know how to tell You what they are doing to me.

According to Your servant Paul, "the Spirit comes to help us, weak as we are. For we do not know how we ought to pray; the Spirit himself pleads with God for us in groans that words cannot express. And God who sees into our hearts, knows what the thought of the Spirit is, because the Spirit pleads with God on behalf of his people and in accordance with his will."

That is great, God! Now, God, listen to the Spirit. Please listen to the Spirit.

Discipline Is Beneficial

Sometimes prayers come so easily that we sense we could not prevent them if we tried. Speaking to God seems like the most natural, effortless act in the world. Supreme happiness floods our souls, and almost instinctively we declare, "Thank God!" or "Thanks be to God." Likewise, when we battle fear, scuffle with perplexity, edge near despair, or try to escape trouble, the whisper of a prayer, maybe even a prayerful shout, appears virtually unstoppable. "Help me, God!" "O God, I need you!" In such situations, not to pray is more unthinkable than to pray.

At other times, though, prayer looks like a totally unnecessary, bothersome interruption. Devoid of critical fluctuations, life moves along at a rather steady pace. No major happiness excites us, and no dreadful problem worries us. Playing the role of captains of our fate, we claim to have a handle on everything and we boast of doing well. *Why pray?* we think. *I have everything under control.*

Many love affairs disintegrate during periods when one or both of the lovers decide (consciously or unconsciously) that keeping a busy schedule of appointments must take priority over communion with the other person. Because we don't have our priorities properly focused and we confuse productive busyness (or business) with meaningful living, we lose touch with our need for loving communion. In relation to God, prayer may be more important during these times than in any others.

C. S. Lewis wrote of his great difficulty in keeping regular times of prayer. Though Lewis affirmed the importance of persistent prayer, he admitted looking for almost any excuse to avoid praying. Not unlike some of us, probably, the great British writer confessed that he allowed virtually any noise to distract him from praying. However, Lewis observed that he had to say his prayers regularly if he intended to go on living, even as he had to study grammar regularly if he was to continue reading poetry.[2]

Persistent prayer requires discipline, as do love and love affairs. However, the discipline of prayer (and of love) is not an act of confinement or punishment but an invitation to intimacy, freedom, and unparalleled joy.

What about Schedules?

Many people find great benefit in keeping scheduled times of prayer. Long ago the Roman Catholic Church and the Eastern Orthodox Church formalized stated times for both public and private prayers to be offered in the course of a day. This practice of establishing "canonical hours" (the specified times for daily prayers) reaches far back into early Christianity when believers engaged in public prayers at dawn and at sunset.[3]

Some individuals rigidly observe a personal schedule for daily prayers—rising early in the morning to pray from 6:00 a.m. to 6:30 a.m. while all is quiet in the house; designating an hour after lunch each day in their office to read, meditate, and pray; protecting thirty minutes of solitude for prayer before going to bed every night. At one point in his life, Howard Thurman resolved, "I am conditioning my nervous system so that after tonight, until the end of the journey, it will be impossible for me inadvertently to step out of bed onto the floor without first making a circle of light to guide me."[4]

Scheduled times for communion with God can enhance our prayer lives. Warnings are in order, however.

I know two lovers who lead incredibly busy lives. Realizing that their relationship would suffer from a lack of time spent together in meaningful communion, these lovers wisely designated one hour late each evening to sit together and talk. They agreed that regardless of the press of other matters, every night at this time they would stop what they were doing and meet for conversation. Each kept the agreement. But a problem surfaced. More times than not, each came to the designated hour wrung out by the demands of the day, preoccupied with what remained undone, and eager to lie down and rest. Both kept their schedule faithfully, but neither experienced a bonding-type of communion with the other.

Praying just to keep a schedule differs radically from praying to communicate with God. These two motivations for prayer may coincide, but not necessarily. People eager to pray on a regular schedule can go through the motions of prayer at specified times each day without ever seriously communing with God. For spiritual lovers, meaningful communion with God and growth in love requires much more than a schedule.

If scheduling encourages prayer, fine. However, I know of no moment in which meaningful prayer cannot occur. Claiming time alone for extended silence and carefully thought-out prayers benefits me greatly. But I can pray on the run. I have experienced profound times of prayer while walking down a hospital corridor, in the midst of a counseling session, and while driving to a crucial meeting.

God is like a personal lover, but not identical to one. God is the Divine Lover. Time and space do not limit God. As the psalmist so eloquently instructs us, we cannot go anywhere in all creation that takes us beyond the presence of God (Ps. 139). Thus, communion with God can occur at any place in any moment.

When schedules help us commune with God, they serve a wonderful purpose. However, when schedules load us down with legalistic baggage and restrict our communion with God, we had best get rid of them. Responding to God's call for persistence in prayer involves not keeping a punctual schedule but enjoying intimacy with a (the) unique Lover.

At its best, all of life constitutes a prayer to God. No moment stands apart from or outside our love affair with God.

When God Is Silent

I used to think that God always answers prayers with either "yes," "no," or "wait a while." (Interestingly, this assumes that all prayers ask something of God.) For a while this simple formula satisfied me. Eventually, though, as I thought about my experiences and listened to stories from other people, I concluded that some prayers receive no specific answer from God. At times, God seems to be deaf to our prayers and silent about answers.

A young girl sat talking to her pastor, recounting a traumatic episode in her life a few days earlier. An older man had attacked and molested her. After recalling that throughout the time the man was mistreating her she was praying for help, the troubled child abruptly ended her story with a penetrating question: "Why didn't Jesus answer me?"

A Historical Problem

The unsettling inquiry represents far more than the desperate cry of an innocent little girl caught up in the sin in a man's life. Questions about God's silence have been voiced throughout history.

The prophet Habakkuk screamed at God more than once—first asking, "O LORD, how long shall I cry for help and you will not listen?" (1:2), and then "Why do you look on the treacherous, and are silent when the wicked swallow those more righteous than they?" (1:13). The prophet Isaiah emphatically asserted, "Truly, you are a God who hides himself" (45:15).

At one point during the Reformation, Martin Luther pleaded with God, "O Lord God, punish us, but be not silent toward us."[5] In the midst of World War II, historian H. G. Wells described God as "an ever-absent help in time of trouble."[6] More recently, before the breakup of the

Soviet Union, a Russian Orthodox priest wrote, "Here we are, God's servants, waiting, waiting, and nothing happens. The heavens are silent, the stars are silent, everything is silent."[7]

Most of us know this historical problem from personal experience. After periods of sincere praying, we have felt the chill of an eerie silence or, worse still, watched a worsening of the situation which first prompted our prayers for help. Then, from an office suite, a hospital room, the site of an accident, or somewhere else, we have joined our voices to those before us asking, "Why? Why, God? Why are You silent?"

O God, the silence is scaring me.

Maybe I just function better amid noise. But, I don't think so. I really need to hear from You.

I am being asked questions for which I have no answers.

I am trying to make decisions with no clear understanding of the consequences involved.

I can't make any sense out of much of the suffering all around me.

I don't see why my efforts at peacemaking end up causing more conflict.

And I am tired of silence.

God, I know, I know that sometimes I have trouble hearing when You speak. I even know why. I don't always want to hear Your words because I don't always like what I hear.

But, now, I need to hear from You.

Too much silence has been present for too long.

Please speak God. Please speak to me. Please let me hear from You. Become words again. And make the words become flesh. Then, don't ever stop.

Keep on speaking.

I'm listening, God. I'm listening.

An Attempt at Explanations

In some situations, no satisfactory explanations for God's silence emerge. However, on other occasions, we can discern possible reasons for God's hiddenness. Each instance of God's apparent silence must be evaluated separately.

Situations arise when our spiritual deafness, not God's terrible silence, is the problem. We may accuse God of detachment when in reality we are the ones in a far country. God gets blamed for more than God deserves.

God's revelations seldom overpower us. God speaks in subtle ways—through a still, small voice whispered in a sunset, through a brisk autumn afternoon, or on a fresh spring morning. Sometimes God addresses us through other people—colleagues at work, friends in our church, social acquaintances, or family members. To recognize God's voice, we must be sensitive to God's voice. Otherwise, we may charge God with silence at the very moment God speaks to us.

Occasionally, our search for God's voice ends in futility because we seek a god who does not exist. As long as we look for a god shaped in our image, we never will find the true God. The God revealed in Jesus Christ refuses to be bound by our expectations.

Some folks listen for the voice of a god who can only say yes to what they do, while others seek a god programmed to speak in negatives. Some people desire a god far removed from and totally unaffected by this life, while others demand to hear from a god who has forfeited every dimension of transcendence in favor of total immersion in the contemporary situation. Some people pursue a god who knows only love without wrath, while others seek a deity always inclined to anger rather than compassion. Some individuals want a god who explains life in its most minute details, while others long for a god who cares nothing at all for knowledge. All such safaris end in disappointment and give rise to observations about God's silence.

Sometimes periods of apparent silence from God relate directly to improper attitudes among God's people. Do we not at times pursue God or listen for God only because we have something we want to tell God or ask God? I know I do. Far more times than I want to admit, I have approached God . . . not to find the divine will and covenant to obey it, but to secure God's endorsement of an agreement drawn up on my terms.

Often our complaints about God's silence reveal attitudes, actions, and words which prevent us from perceiving anyone else's words and will. We so eagerly posture ourselves to address God that we fail to hear God addressing us. We become so totally engrossed in efforts to lead God that we miss opportunities to be led by God.

Two Case Studies

Job. The Old Testament character named Job struggled to understand the adversities which filled his life: Why do good people suffer? Why do evil people seem to prosper more than good people? Where can I find security? How can I discover comfort?

Eventually Job decided that God was behind everything that had happened to him and concluded that God owed him an explanation. But God was silent.

Job prayed. Oh my, how he prayed! In fact, Job grew weary of praying and waiting to hear God's responsive voice. Finally, fed up with his situation, Job resolved that since God would not volunteer some word for him, he would wring a word out of God. Lifting his fist into the air defiantly as if to shake it in the face of God, Job challenged God: "Let the Almighty answer me!" (31:35).

149

Once the echo of Job's cries receded, silence shrouded the sufferer like a heavy fog. After all his kicking and screaming, complaining and pleading, God had not said a mumbling word to Job. That was it. Job was at the end of his rope—finished. Right there, though, something happened which prepared Job to hear God speak.

Job finally arrived at a point where he was ready to hear God speak, not on his terms but on God's terms. Job decided that he even could be content living with mystery if God would only indicate that mystery was the divine intention for his life. The author of the Book of Job succinctly, but dramatically, described the exact moment at which Job's attitude changed to the point that God could answer his prayers: "The words of Job are ended" (31:40). Job fell silent.

Not everyone who reads the Book of Job agrees that God answered Job. I read the biblical narrative a long time before I saw God's answer. But God's response came. "The LORD answered Job out of the whirlwind," the author declared (38:1). What Job received from God exceeded what Job bargained for.

God responded to Job through God's creation, setting before Job the vastness and greatness of the created order. God helped Job see himself as only a small part of creation, a finite being limited in his understanding of the ways of God. Then God said no more to Job.

True, God did not provide detailed answers to any of Job's questions—none of them. God offered not a single word of explanation regarding Job's sufferings or a vindication of Job's righteousness. I searched in vain for such divine responses. Just as I was about to give up on ever understanding how God answered Job out of the whirlwind, I caught sight of an incredibly important truth: God answered Job! God spoke, and Job got the message.

God responded to Job's prayers with a gift of the Divine Presence. God gave Job what he needed rather than what he wanted. No, Job did not get what he requested. He got more. Nothing in life equals in importance the realization of God's presence—an awareness that we live and move within the Divine Presence whose essential nature is love.

Though Job had no explanation of the events which had altered his life, he had the promise of God's presence in all the events of his life. Job's unanswered questions became meaningless. God's answer to Job's prayers was God's presence in Job's life.

Paul. Paul's prayers about his "thorn in the flesh" reinforced the truth I discovered in the narratives on Job. Paul indicated that on three occasions he prayed to God about a major problem in his life, implying that he asked God to remove the difficulty from him. However, God neither took away the problem nor explained why.

God did speak to Paul, though. The apostle heard the divine declaration, "My grace is sufficient for you" (2 Cor. 12:9). And that was enough—more than enough, actually. God promised to be with Paul and to surround his human weakness with divine strength. What more could the apostle ask? If I have to choose between dealing with a difficulty out of my own weakness and experiencing God's gift of grace, I will choose grace every time.

Amid our complaints and grumblings about God's silence, we best remember the experiences of Job and Paul. Stilling the impulse to scream at God, "Why will You not answer me?" or to fight with God, we realize that God responds to us with the greatest gift imaginable—the gift of the Divine Presence full of grace. What a Lover!

Candidly, if at this point we still prefer explanations from God to the constant enjoyment of God's presence, we demonstrate that we are neither smart enough nor wise enough to understand answers to our questions, even if God provided them.

What Should We Do in the Silence?

For whatever reasons, most of us experience times when we feel distance and silence between ourselves and God. What should we do when this happens?

Initially, we may find help by carefully examining our personal spiritual situation in light of the possible explanations for God's silence discussed earlier in this chapter: Am I failing to hear God because I am not listening, or because God is not speaking? Am I looking for a god which is not God? Do I expect God to conform to my expectations before I accept God's disclosures as revelation?

Honestly, sometimes such introspection yields no beneficial insights. Silence remains.

Carlyle Marney liked to tell people who complained of God's silence to live on the basis of the last clear word from God they heard until they could hear another one. Marney's wise counsel has proven helpful to me. Even during periods of spiritual dryness, God's words from the past remain certain: "I am with you always" (Matt. 28:20); "If we confess our sins, he who is faithful and just will forgive us our sins and cleanse us from all unrighteousness" (1 John 1:9); "Peace I leave with you; my peace I give to you" (John 14:27). I can live for a long time in silence on the basis of those kinds of promises, which I know the silence does not destroy.

When I am not exactly sure what God would have me do in the future, I try to act on what God has instructed me to do in the past: "do justice, . . . love kindness, and . . . walk humbly with your God" (Micah 6:8); "be quick to listen, slow to speak, slow to anger" (James 1:19); "love your enemies" (Matt. 5:44); "glorify God" (1 Cor. 6:20).

Faithful love requires that even when waiting to hear a new word from God, we stay busy trying to carry out the directions God has already given us.

Distance between Lovers

That's the way life goes with lovers. Problems with distance or feelings of distance invade even the most intense love affairs. Sometimes the distance is real, maybe even geographical. In that situation, each lover finds strength and comfort in recalling the words exchanged the last time they were together: "I love you. Being apart cannot destroy my love for you." Memory brings reassurance: "God loves me"; "She loves me."

Emotional distance can be every bit as difficult for lovers to handle as geographical distance. When two people have to negotiate a series of difficult, controversial events, not uncommonly an uneasy feeling of distance develops between them. Faced by this troublesome development, lovers recommit themselves to the kind of communion which contributes to intimacy.

In other situations, one lover feels distance, but the other does not. One asks, "What has happened to us? I don't feel the same closeness between us." The other replies, "I feel as close to you as ever. I don't know why you feel such distance. Maybe you have moved away, but I haven't." At that point, the lovers have to work together to find the source of the sense of separation eating away at one of them.

When distance or silence invades our love affair with God, the need for persistent prayer becomes greater than ever. Honestly negotiating a sense of distance from God (like faithfully proceeding during a period of perceived silence from God) can result in an even more profound love for God.

Persistent Love

Lovers do not ask how often they should speak or seek to be together. The love they share renders that question meaningless. They know the joy in communion with each other; they prize constant contact, unbroken fellowship, and continuous communication.

To commune with God means to live in love—to interact with the Ultimate Lover. Why would anyone ever desire less than persistent communion with God?

God's insistence that we pray persistently is not a burdensome obligation, rather it is an invitation to the wonder and joy of an unending love affair.

૨ેન

CHAPTER TEN

Prayer is in the first instance waiting, expecting.

Jurgen Moltmann, *The Passion for Life*

PRAYING EXPECTANTLY

Love births expectations—great expectations. Lovers make promises to each other which provide security in the present and create anticipation for the future. Living on the verge of surprise, lovers peer into the future with vibrant hope.

As two people grow in their love for each other, new dimensions—completely unexpected dimensions—of their love emerge. "I never knew a relationship could be so wonderful!" a woman breathlessly exclaims after an astonishing realization of what her lover means to her. Every new discovery of the depth and breadth of love brings with it the experience of a joy which neither lover could have anticipated at the beginning of their relationship. Each joyous surprise—or surprise of joy—among lovers greatly enhances their positive expectations related to the future.

The great German theologian Karl Barth viewed all Christian prayer as "radically eschatalogical"—"an eschatalogical cry based on the acknowledgment of God's name, will, and reign."[1] Barth's belief about prayer reflects the kind of expectancy which forms the heartbeat of a love affair, especially a love affair with God. Communion with God causes us to face forward. Waiting and hoping go hand-in-hand with praying. The more we know about God and experience God's love, the more expectantly we pray to God as lovers.

Looking Back to See Ahead

For a long time, I mistakenly associated hope only with the future. That kind of hope fails to offer much help. A hope oriented exclusively to the future has no substance; it is more akin to a fervent wish than to a realistic expectation. Helpful hope looks as much to the past as to the future. Memory produces hope.

Remembering how God repeatedly delivered the people of Israel from bondage gives me hope as I face difficulty in the present. I am encouraged from biblical stories which recount God's redemptive actions on behalf of folks troubled by doubts and temptations. When the residue of old sins causes me to wonder if I can ever be free of guilt, I find comfort recalling God's ministry of forgiveness through the ages. At the center of the biblical message stands an unmistakable conclusion: God keeps promises!

Throughout the Scriptures, authors repeat the rhythm of promise and fulfillment. The Old Testament preserves tale after tale of God keeping promises to people who broke promises. And, of course, the New Testament conveys the good news of divine promises fulfilled: "The Word became flesh and lived among us" (John 1:14); "While we still were sinners, Christ died for us" (Rom. 5:8).

Like the people of God before us, we can find hope for the future by remembering the past. This hope, unlike an empty wish flung into the wind, rests upon a solid conviction about the promise-keeping nature of the Divine Lover. Lovers of God who pray with an active memory, pray about the future expectantly. Informed by the past, we can speak to God with specific hopes for the future and certain assurances about the present.

Acceptance

Lovers need never worry about being acceptable in each other's presence. When true to its nature, love dictates the acceptance of one lover by another. No conditions. No exceptions.

Periodically, most of us speak to God with hesitation, or maybe even embarrassment: "God, I hate to bother You with this, but I am in a situation that is killing me. I knew better than to get involved in this thing. It's wrong. But I am in way over my head. I need help. Could You possibly understand and help me? Or, are You so disgusted with me that You will not even listen to me?"

God assures us of acceptance, not affirmation, agreement, or endorsement, but acceptance. God loves us and wants to hear from us—when we are at our worst as well as when we are at our best, when we are weakest as well as when we are strong, when we are "down" as well as when we are "up." God welcomes all our prayers and accepts us as we pray them.

Jesus issued a timeless invitation born of the divine love which encompasses us: "Come to me, all you that are weary and are carrying heavy burdens, and I will give you rest" (Matt. 11:28). Count on it! We can never be too fatigued, too worried, too dirty, or too sinful for God to accept us. Even when God disdains the reasons for our neediness, God accepts us in our times of need. We can never be so far removed from God that God will not welcome us back into the Divine Presence. Even when God grieves over our self-determined distance and separation from all that is holy, God readily welcomes our return to communion.

Assured of God's acceptance, we pray expectantly. Something good, something helpful, something redemptive can come from every occasion of communion with the Holy Lover.

Forgiveness

"But what about sin? How can God accept us in spite of our sins?" a hurting man asks, anxiously watching his whole life come apart because of wrongdoing. The good news is that God provided the remedy for our sin. Only the intensity of God's eagerness to forgive exceeds the intensity of God's readiness to hear our requests for forgiveness. God's love will not be thwarted by our evil. Separation from God because of personal immorality is a decision on our part, not an indication of God's inability to accept and forgive us.

No love affair remains immune to infidelity, betrayal, anger, hurt, or some other destructive development. Those things which have the potential to destroy a relationship reveal, as does nothing else, the strength of the love between those involved. Numb from shock, reeling with pain, sick from disappointment, or irate with anger, an offended lover continues to speak with the offender, trying hard to understand what happened, working to avoid bitter retaliation, and hoping to find a way to express forgiveness. Equally as wrong as an act of infidelity between lovers is a willingness to allow that infidelity to destroy their love. An expression of penitence followed by a response of forgiveness can preserve a love affair and actually strengthen the love within it even amid the hurt of infidelity.

God, who will never be the unfaithful partner in a love affair, refuses to allow acts of our sinfulness to destroy the continuation of a love affair with us. Rather than turning away from us, God turns toward us, urges penitence from us, and promises us forgiveness. In the New Testament, in fact, Jesus often portrays a God so ready to forgive penitent people that confessions of sin are encouraged. (The story of the father's reaction to the return of his wayward son in Luke 15:11–24 reflects the same eagerness to bestow forgiveness as that contained in Jesus' prayer from the cross recorded in Luke 23:34: "Father, forgive them; for they do not know what they are doing.")

God accepts us when we seem least acceptable. Again, no exceptions. Our Lover will not turn away from us because of our wrongdoing for which we seek forgiveness. Even at our worst, we can commune with God and expect good to come from the communion.

Grace

Everything we know about God points to the dominance of grace. The history of Israel as told in the Old Testament dramatizes God's penchant for mercy. Time and time again, God responds to people's disobedience with new directions, relates to national infidelity with unwavering personal love, and offers forgiveness to wrongdoers. Even God's judgment expresses God's grace.

Should any question about the importance of God's grace remain, the New Testament answers it decisively. The Gospel of John describes Jesus—the supreme revelation of God—as the One from whom ("from his fullness") we receive "grace upon grace" (John 1:16). The apostle Paul explores the radical consequences of that truth declaring that "while we still were sinners Christ died for us" (Rom. 5:8). In the crucifixion of Jesus, God continued a long-established pattern, revealing as never before what divine grace does with the sins of humanity: "Where sin increased, grace abounded all the more" (Rom. 5:20).

The operative word is *grace*—a term which explains why God loves us when we are unlovable and prepares for our forgiveness even before we move to repentance. Stripped to its essence, *grace* means an unexpected and undeserved gift. The term *grace* applies to unmerited initiatives for good, God's redemptive action on behalf of the undeserving. God's grace assures us that no circumstance in our lives can take us beyond the reach of God's love and the possibility of communion with the Divine Lover.

Grace exudes power. Grace is far more than a passive biblical concept: it enters the world as a transforming force. God's grace turns despicable occasions of evil into memorable opportunities for redemption. No situation ever gets so bad that grace cannot make it better. Addressed by grace, dark despair gives way to enlightening hope.

Love and mercy accompany grace. Each of the three looks just like the other two. Frequently someone calls grace "love" or "mercy" or vice versa. No problem. God is love; God is grace; God is mercy. The God whom we know as Lover or Beloved fills our love affair with grace. We can count on it.

A look at God's "grace-full" actions in the past instills within us great confidence for the future! No wonder we as lovers of God, pray expectantly.

Growth

Delays inevitably develop in love affairs. Not every moment can be filled with joyful closeness and realized expectations. Lovers face the challenge of continuing to trust each other and to nurture intimacy when dreams and cherished hopes threaten to fade.

At this point, lovers of God do well to remember the past. God dominates in-between-times as well as times of creation and end-times. Longing for the flood to end, Noah discovered God riding out the high water with him. Yearning for the promised land, the people of Israel experienced God's generous mercy in a wilderness. During centuries of eager waiting for the arrival of the Messiah, God's people developed a trust in God which gave confidence to their hope.

While waiting for some specific action on God's part, we develop and exercise spiritual muscles which we never would even discover if all our requests to God received immediate responses. Deferred dreams need not discourage love. Whatever we are waiting for, we do not have to delay nurturing our love for God or celebrating the certainty of God's promises.

Love affairs not only survive difficult times of unfulfilled hopes, distance between lovers, and problems which appear to have no quick solutions, often they actually mature during such periods. Rather than giving up on each other, thoughtful lovers work harder than ever at nurturing their relationship. A time of waiting becomes a time of significant growth in love. And expectations rooted in the love affair not only survive but flourish.

Realistic Expectations and Useless Prayers

Lovers expect a lot from each other. However, love itself prevents us from imposing unrealistic demands upon one another. As our Lover, God never leads us into situations or calls us to tasks which we cannot handle. Likewise, as lovers of God, we restrict the content of our prayers to concerns which interest God and to requests which God wills to answer. Though the love between God and us frees us to talk about anything and everything, the discipline and respect which are so much a part of our love for God silence irrelevant, useless words on our part.

Irrelevant Prayers

The final score of an athletic event bears no real consequences for the love that bonds two people together. Communion within a love affair transcends any sporting competition's designation of winners and losers. God leaves the outcome of ball games and other matches of athletic skills to the participants involved and their conduct within each competition.

We talk to our lover (human or Divine) about our wishes, intentions, and feelings related to most everything we care about. Approaching a major sports event, we may share our excitement about it and our hopes for its outcome. But we don't expect our lover to determine the final score of the competition, nor do we rest the future of our love affair on who wins and loses according to a scoreboard.

Often before my personal involvement in an athletic event, I have asked God to help me do my best, to enable me to stay focused, and to deliver me from major injury. But I don't ask God to allow me to win or to cause my opponent to lose. God has far more important work to do than become involved in designating winners and losers in the stadiums and gymnasiums of the world.

Asking God what style of furniture to purchase or how to landscape a yard falls into the same category as praying to win a ball game. It's a waste of time. What I do with my money is important, but whether I buy a red chair or a yellow chair matters little to God. Why ask for divine assistance in making a choice which has no bearing at all on my love affair with God?

Perhaps the singular most irrelevant prayer I have ever encountered came from a woman genuinely worried about a fictional character on a soap opera which she faithfully watched on television. This lady asked friends to join her in praying for a successful surgery for a non-entity, an unreal individual with no life beyond the plot development of an imaginative script writer.

Impossible Requests

Frankly, some prayers ought never be prayed. By their very nature, the petitions have no place within a love affair. Consider two examples.

Late one night, after several continuous hours of work, I prompted my word processor to delete a major section of material for this book. I did not mean to do it. In fact, only after I had proceeded to a point at which the material could no longer be retrieved did I realize what I had done. Instinctively, I found myself beginning to pray, "God, help me get it back. I've worked so conscientiously, please overcome my stupidity and make the words reappear on the screen in front of me." It was a useless prayer. I had made a major mistake. God could help me deal with the consequences of my error, but God could not be expected to change the fact that I had activated the delete command on my computer.

As a couple drives into the neighborhood in which they live, they spot a large plume of dark black smoke billowing into the sky over a location which appears to be close to their house. No sooner does she see the signs of a fire than the wife blurts out a prayer, "O God, please don't let that be our house on fire." She offers a needless petition.

A house is already on fire; the blaze can be seen from a distance. Either the woman's house is going up in flames or it isn't; it's too late to alter which house is on fire.

Despite the breadth and depth of God's love for us and the omnipotence of God's nature, God cannot answer these kinds of prayers.

Harsh and Hurtful Prayers

God welcomes praise and thanksgiving; indeed, God delights in both. But God rejects expressions of gratitude based upon the superiority of one person over another or the affluence which one individual enjoys at the expense of poverty among others. Remember Jesus' critical attitude toward the Pharisee who prayed aloud, "God, I thank you that I am not like other people" (Luke 18:11).

Most of us have been tempted to offer such a prayer to God even if we have defeated the temptation—"God, I am so thankful that I have really good health when so many of my friends are in and out of hospitals regularly"; or, "God, thank You for blessing our nation with abundance and making us strong in a world of starvation and need." God takes no delight in these kinds of prayers.

Actually, according to the Old Testament, God finds chauvinistic declarations of praise offensive—transgressions against the divine will. The prophet Amos pointed a finger of judgment at people who sang songs of praise to God because of clothing which had been taken from a neighbor (2:8). Likewise he warned his listeners that when they adored God while taking advantage of their neighbors, they actually profaned God rather than glorified God (2:7–8; 4:5).

God loves the whole world. Anytime our communion with God takes place in isolation from, or as a substitute for, interaction with our neighbors, God nullifies our prayer. God refuses to listen to expressions of gratitude for personal successes achieved through the abuse, misuse, neglect, manipulation, or depersonalization of others.

As Patrick Miller so convincingly points out, under some circumstances the praise of God gets the offerers of that praise in serious trouble. Praise to God for gains which we enjoy because of others' losses prompts God's anger and damnation rather than commendation and appreciation.[2] Amos heralded the unambiguous message of God in such situations: "Take away from me the noise of your songs; I will not listen to the melody of your harps. But let justice roll down like waters, and righteousness like an everflowing stream" (5:23–24).

Tests of Love

No lover appreciates contrived tests of his or her love. Certainly not God.

Prayers which attempt to test God, to force God to prove the divine nature, displease God. A troubled man prays, "God, if You really love me, You will get me out of this mess so I can better serve You." A grieving mother throws down a gauntlet, "God, if You don't make my baby well, I will doubt Your mercy forever." Each statement places a condition upon which a relationship with God will be considered.

Any prayer aimed at forcing a demonstration of God's love for us as a prerequisite for our loving and serving God misses the whole point of prayer and reflects a gross misunderstanding of the nature of God and personal faith. God is not a barterer, a horse trader, a connoisseur of shop-and-swap spirituality. God is love. God loves us—all of us—already. If anything is in question in prayer, it is not God's love for us but our response to God's love. Besides, how much sense does it make to ask God to prove the very attribute which makes our prayers possible in the first place or to demand that God do what God has been doing since the beginning of time?

Praying expectantly must be distinguished from wishing fervently, practicing blind hope, or practicing some kind of voodooish magic. Prayer is not a handy means of getting everything we want from God. Prayer is communion between lovers—no more, but no less. Speaking to our Lover, we consciously decide that some matters simply have no place in our prayers.

Patient Waiting

Love requires patience, as does a life of expectant prayer. Love stirs excitement and starts adrenaline flowing. Patience looks like a hindrance to love's eagerness to get on with everything, at least at first. Lovers can hardly wait to share new experiences, learn more about each other, and taste all the delights of communion—in other words, to grow together in their love. But love takes time. The fullest realizations of the joy of love do not come quickly. Lovers learn patience; they have to.

So do pray-ers. Our requests to God do not always result in immediate fulfillment. Sometimes generations pass before God's promises come to fruition in the world. Everybody goes through periods in which God's will seems delayed, if not stifled. Patience wears thin. But continued communion with our Lover saves us from despair.

Patience between lovers derives strength and receives nurture not from events but from the trust in each other born of the love carried within them. Far more than baseless optimism or reckless wishful thinking, trust between lovers rests on the solid foundation of historical precedent and personal experience.

We look forward to God's reign arriving and God's will prevailing because of specific, historical, biblically recorded incidents of divine revelation, not because of fanciful pipe dreams. We know what has happened already—the triumph of love in Bethlehem, the victory won by our Lover on a hill called Calvary, the resilience of love demonstrated in the face of death beside a garden tomb in Jerusalem. The sovereignty of God in history and the sufficiency of God for redemption are not in question.

Dreadful skirmishes with evil continue. Lesser kingdoms and lords appear to prevail from time to time. However, the nature of the end of it all is not in doubt. Out of our communion with God now, we look to the future with a confidence shaped by the past. God's kingdom comes and will come. God's will prevails; God's will will be done.

Many of my prayers reflect both waiting (not always patiently) and hoping.

God, I have all these needs—
> unanswered questions,
> unencouraged convictions,
> unaffirmed ministries,
> unapplauded courage, and
> undirected decisions.

I really do need to hear from You—to hear Your answers, to hear Your expressions of encouragement, affirmation, applause, and direction. Right now, though, all seems quiet, much too quiet. Amid the silence which surrounds my needs, I remember Your promises. God, You have made a lot of promises. And, right now I want to claim them.

You promised that You would work in all things for good for those who love You. I claim that promise now.

You promised a faith strong enough to move mountains and durable enough to sustain us in all situations. I claim that promise now.

You promised that Your Word would have a redemptive ministry in our lives. I claim that promise now.

You promised that if we make requests of You from our belief in You that You will hear us and respond. I claim that promise now.

God, thank You for the many ways in which I can speak to You and for the variety of ways in which You speak to me. Right now, though, thank You for the ministry of Your good promises and for the faithfulness with which You keep them.

While learning patience, lovers discover a great surprise. Waiting for the arrival of a longed-for future does not preclude growing in love in the present. Remember the inspired promise of the prophet Isaiah: "Those who wait for the LORD shall renew their strength, they shall mount up with wings like eagles, they shall run and not be weary, they shall walk and not faint" (40:31).

Not uncommonly, the love between two lovers grows to new levels of maturity more while they are waiting expectantly for promises to be fulfilled than while they busily celebrate dreams that have come true.

We may actually learn to love God more as we learn to wait on God patiently and expectantly.

Taking Action

Lovers usually talk with each other about what they are doing. Similarly, the subjects of our prayers usually grow out of, as well as become the objects of, our actions.

Patient waiting need not keep us from taking action aimed at helping solve problems about which we are praying. If we care enough about a situation to pray about it, we care enough about it to work on it. Our prayerful expectation that the ultimate resolution of a particular difficulty may not be known until sometime in a distant future should not prevent us from doing everything in our power to eliminate this difficulty in the present.

A Biblical Pattern

Two sentences set side-by-side in the prayer which Jesus taught God's disciples to pray represent a "parallelism" common in Jewish literature. The first line and the second line share essentially the same meaning; the second line provides additional insight into the definition of the first line. Jesus prayed:

Your kingdom come.
Your will be done,
 on earth as it is in heaven. (Matt. 6:10)

The first petition represents an expectant request—anticipating the coming of God's kingdom. Jesus prayed, "Let your kingdom come." Then, in God's very next statement, Jesus offered the same request in a different manner, verbalizing a petition which defined the meaning of the coming kingdom: "Your will be done, on earth as it is in heaven." Place the two lines together and you understand that people doing God's will on earth signals the arrival of God's kingdom.

Jesus' request "Your kingdom come" implies patient waiting. However, God's repetition of that request—"Your will be done"—implies purposeful action. The two belong together. Jesus prayed for God's will to be done in the redemption of the world, then picked up a cross and trudged toward His death. For us, doing the will of God means sharing the gospel, reconciling enemies, stilling violence, feeding the hungry, seeking peace, aiding the poor, housing the homeless, doing justice, practicing kindness, and demonstrating mercy (e.g., Micah 6:8; Matt. 25:32–45) in addition to speaking with God about all these concerns. To pray sincerely for God's will to be done in our world means dedicating ourselves to the doing of God's will in our lives.

Few of our prayers include the kind of parallelism found in the Lord's Prayer. However, seeking to do God's will with our lives always parallels asking for God's will to be done in our prayers. When we pray honestly and expectantly, we act on what we pray about.

A Historical Pattern

In every age, truly pious people have combined expectant prayers with influential actions. Moses prayed to God about the enslavement of the Hebrew people, then committed himself to lead these slaves out of Egypt. The apostle Paul prayed for the salvation of the Gentiles as he unselfishly gave himself to that gospel mission.

The closer we get to God in communion the more immersed we become in serving—God and other people.

Expectation and Action. In the latter part of the eighteenth century, a humble English cobbler by the name of William Carey became convicted about the need to share the gospel around the world. Carey studied the Bible with great discipline and served as a lay preacher. He prayed about the need for a foreign missions movement among Baptists and, though extremely shy, pleaded openly with his Baptist colleagues to begin such an enterprise. From his post as the pastor of a local congregation, Carey developed a simple strategy for involving Baptists in a program of worldwide evangelism—pray, plan, and pay.[3]

During a Baptist meeting in Nottingham, England, on May 31, 1792, Carey preached a powerful sermon based upon Isaiah 54:2–3. He trumpeted an admonition about missions which succinctly encapsulated the encouragement of this chapter regarding prayer: "Expect great things from God; attempt great things for God."

William Carey prayed for an international missionary movement among Baptists. He also labored long and hard for the development of such an initiative. Carey's work prompted more prayer, and his prayers led to more work. As a direct result of William Carey's efforts, the Baptist Missionary Society formed in October of 1792. During the following year, Carey and his family set sail for India as foreign missionaries. William Carey practiced what he preached and preached what he practiced. In relation to God, expect and attempt; in service to God, pray, plan, and participate. Carey committed his life to helping God answer the prayerful request which he repeatedly had set before God.

Devotion and Liberation. John Woolman served as an agent for social revolution in colonial America, challenging the evil institution of slavery. But few people thought of Woolman as a social reformer; his identity and ministry exemplified quiet Christian piety. Woolman's influence in society related directly to his devotion to God. A belief in the inclusive nature of God's love and a practice of unceasing prayer surrounded this Quaker's critique of slavery.

In his personal journal, Woolman often wrote of feeling "covered with the spirit of prayer."[4] He viewed the place of prayer as "a precious habitation."[5] Woolman repeatedly prayed for the guidance of God's will in his own life as well as for God's help in the lives of the black slaves and Indians whose plights he wanted to improve. When controversy swirled around this humble man and critics denigrated him and his work, Woolman prayed more fervently for the peace which comes from God alone: "My cries of help were put up to the Lord, who, in great mercy, gave me a resigned heart, in which I found quietness."[6]

John Woolman's compassionate efforts to establish justice grew out of his prayers of devotion. In turn, Woolman's tireless labor on behalf of human liberation prompted still more prayers. Such a marriage of talk and work represents the quality of communion which belongs in a love affair between God and all of us.

Prayer and Compassion. Few people have impacted the world for good more profoundly than a small in stature, giant in spirit, nun known as Mother Teresa. Since she began picking up dying people in the streets of Calcutta, India, back in 1952, Mother Teresa and members of the Missionaries of Society (which she founded) have demonstrated the love of God in Christ to hundreds of thousands of abandoned, homeless persons.

Unquestionably an activist, Mother Teresa models a life of prayer suitable for a solely contemplative person and admonishes all who work alongside her to "love to pray."[7] Mother Teresa explains her ministry to the dying as action born of a love for Jesus. "I do this because I believe I am doing it for Jesus," she confesses.[8] "If we pray the work . . . if we do it to Jesus, if we do it for Jesus, if we do it with Jesus . . . that's what makes us content."[9]

Mother Teresa's prayers reveal the secret of her powerful ministry. She looks to God for the source, direction, and strength of her work. "Make us worthy, Lord, to serve our fellow men throughout the world who live and die in poverty and hunger," Mother Teresa prays. "Give them through our hands this day their daily bread, and by our understanding love, give peace and joy."[10]

Revealing the depths of both her compassion for hurting people and her love for God, this amazing little nun constantly communes with God about those she helps. Mother Teresa prays generally, "Let them look up and see no longer us but only Jesus." And, in that same spirit, she prays more specifically: "Let us preach you without preaching not by words, but by our example by the catching force the sympathetic influence of what we do the evident fullness of the love our hearts bear to you."[11]

A Personal Conviction

All of us should pray about situations over which we have no control, to which we can make no personal contribution by our actions. But we have no right to only pray about circumstances which we can improve by means of our involvement in them. Sincere prayers concerning matters we can personally do something about lead to actions aimed at improving the causes of our concern. When we help alleviate a problem, salve a hurt, or establish good, our deeds become an extension of our prayers—each deed constitutes an action form of prayer.

A few years ago, I began concluding my prayers of intercession and requests with a comment such as, "God, help me to work in such a manner that I can bring about at least a partial answer to my prayer" or "God, use me in answering this prayer." Saying these words to God keeps me aware of my personal responsibility in relation to situations about which I pray and prods me to action. Recently, I learned that the famed English martyr of the sixteenth century, Sir Thomas More, liked to offer a similar prayer: "The things, good Lord, that I pray for, give me your grace to labor for."[12] Amen!

Our prayers lead to actions just as our actions give content to our prayers. And frequently our actions serve as prayers—loving communion with God. Nicholas Grou observed that every action carried out in the sight of God "because it is the will of God, and in the manner that God wills, is a prayer and indeed a better prayer than could be made in words at such times."[13]

Wait, Work, and Watch

Expectant praying signals a growing love for God. To pray expectantly means to wait patiently, to work diligently, and to watch hopefully. God's promises will be fulfilled. For that fulfillment we wait. Great expanses of time may separate a particular promise from its moment of fulfillment. But future fulfillment is as certain as the fact that the promise has been made. Vincent van Gogh offered sound advice: "Let him who believes in God wait for the hour that will come sooner or later."[14]

God's work must continue even while we wait for God's promises to be fulfilled. God's work keeps us busy. Henri Nouwen properly observes, "Action and prayer are two aspects of the same discipline. Both require that we be present to the suffering world . . . and that we respond to the specific needs of those who make up our world."[15]

God's kingdom comes. For that kingdom we watch. No time limits dictate the length of our looking for it. No signs can tell us of the exact historical moment to which we should devote our attention.

Alongside our expectations of God stands an important expectation regarding ourselves—that, come what may, we will remain committed to Christ and consistent in our communion with God. That is the nature of a real love affair.

Lovers enter a relationship with each other for the long haul. Whether waiting on God, working with God, or watching for God, we continue to speak to God. A seventeenth-century writer named Augustine Baker captured this unwavering intention regarding communication which we sometimes voice as a commitment and at other times speak of in terms of hope: "If I were to live for millions of years, yet would I ever remain thy faithful servant and lover."[16]

≈

The wind of God is always blowing,
but you must hoist your sail.

Fénelon

STAYING IN LOVE WITH GOD

God invites us into a love affair like no other. No sooner do we accept God's invitation than we discover a love which seems too good to be true—a love which, once experienced, forces a redefinition of "good" and "love." Immediately, God accepts us (we let out a deep sigh of relief), lavishes grace upon us (we feel surprise), instills hope within us (a smile spreads across our soul, if not our face), and makes unbroken communion with God possible (gratitude fills our heart).

We respond to God's love with love—our love with God. This love also knows no equals. We find ourselves passionately in love with God, thrilled to the core of our being by the promises of this love affair, and eager to spend time in God's presence speaking with God. A previously unexperienced level of intimacy develops in our relationship with God. We feel ourselves more and more committed to God. Within our willingly granted servitude to

God—as strange as it may sound to some—we find a freedom unlike any we have previously known.

Communion with God creates sheer joy. We speak to God unencumbered with thoughts about time, grammar, or posture. No rules about vocabulary, form, place, or content of our prayers restrict us. Intimacy frees us. God wants to hear from us—any time, any place, any way, about anything—and we are ready to speak to God—all the time, everywhere, silently or audibly, about everything.

A love affair with God produces boundless benefits. Self-esteem soars with the assurance of God's love. Security develops, as does significant hopes. Pleasure prevails—"This is the way life should be." Even major challenges look like great opportunities. Lovers of God delight in finding as many ways as possible to demonstrate their love to God.

Will It Last?

"But, will the love last? *Can* such love last?" a skeptic wants to know. God answers those inquiries with a resouding yes! Not even betrayal, disobedience, and rejection halt God's love. God's love endures.

So, what about our love for God? Do love affairs between individuals teach us anything to watch out for in a love affair with God?

Love affairs between persons tend to follow a common pattern. An initial spark of love erupts quickly into a leaping flame. Fueled by white-hot passion, lovers see no challenge too great and no distance too far to prevent their togetherness. Often looking like fools to dispassionate observers, lovers follow their hearts into intense communion, seeking to share everything with each other and to do everything possible to please each other.

Over time, though, things change. Constant togetherness no longer seems as important. Vulnerability loses its luster. Demands and obligations begin to consume the amount of attention which lovers can devote to each other. Emotional fires fizzle.

This dramatic change in a love affair need not mark its termination—just the opposite really. At this very point, lovers have an opportunity to take their love to new depths of meaning and to find in their relationship new dimensions of communion. Tragically, some lovers mistake diminishing passion for vanishing love. If they can't constantly experience the radical desire, surging needs, and intense emotions, they assume something must be wrong and conclude that their love affair must be ending.

No one should expect relational love to maintain the highest peak of its emotional intensity. In the very best of relationships, passion comes and goes. Commitment remains steady, though, as does devotion. Promises stay intact. Devoted lovers exercise their wills alongside their desires. When our desires fail to lead us in the ways of love, our wills guide us into compassionate communion.

The dynamics in a relationship with God are different. Our emotions, intentions, and actions may vary considerably. But God's love remains intense and faithful as well as relentless in its pursuit of communion. In a relationship with God, we often discover the durable qualities of love only after an initial rush of excitement has receded. Working through a period of doubt or an episode of difficulty may end up strengthening love rather than diminishing it. Our love for God reaches new levels of maturity as we realize that meaningful communion with God does not require a relentless emotional high or behavioral perfection, only willful devotion.

How to Keep Love Going

The factors which keep love going are the same as those which get love going. None, though, is more important than communication.

A love affair can survive almost any difficulty as long as the lovers involved remain open to each other and honestly communicate with each other. Remove communication from a love affair, however, and communion rapidly disintegrates. A dissolution of the love affair follows closely behind.

Communion is to a love affair with God what oxygen is to physical existence. Remove communion and all is lost; nurture it and love grows. So does life.

Prayer is another name for this communion. Prayer is communion within a love affair. We keep in touch with God and mature in our relationship with God by means of prayer.

Our love affair with God dictates how we pray to God. Far from rules and regulations, though, God's dictation results in freedom. God wills to join us in a relationship characterized by the kind of liberty which makes intimacy possible. Secure in God's love for us and confident of our love for God, we speak to God honestly, specifically, obediently, persistently, and expectantly. Prayer not only becomes a way of life for us, our way of life becomes a form of prayer to God.

Coming Full Circle

Thankfully, we are not left alone to nurture our relationship with God. God works at this relationship as well. Even when we grow weary or lazy, become doubtful or resentful, get angry or apathetic, God continues to communicate love to us and invite love from us. If we retain any sensitivity at all, God will not allow us to forego the communion which functions as the lifeblood of our love.

A love affair with God begins with the initiative of God's love, grows in response to the perpetual promptings of that love, and continues because God refuses to give up on the lovers involved. At best, our love and prayers constitute responses to God's love. Once we understand that, we fully realize the nature of prayer as the language of a love affair. And once we correctly understand prayer in that manner, our communion with God becomes an ongoing experience of love vibrant with freedom and intimacy.

❧

ENDNOTES

Chapter One: A Helpful Metaphor

1. Markus Barth, *Ephesians: Translation and Commentary on Chapters 4–6* (Garden City, N.Y.: Doubleday & Company, Inc., 1974), 624.

2. Ignace Lepp, *The Psychology of Loving*, trans. Bernard B. Gilligan (New York: The New American Library, Inc., 1963), 215.

3. Richard J. Foster, *Prayer: Finding the Heart's True Home* (Harper San Francisco: 1992), 141.

4. Henri J. M. Nouwen, *The Way of the Heart: Desert Spirituality and Contemporary Ministry* (New York: The Seabury Press, 1981), 75.

5. Ibid., 92.

6. Andrew M. Greeley, *Year of Grace: A Spiritual Journal* (Chicago: The Thomas More Press, 1990), 218. Though Greeley sees life itself as "an invitation to a love affair in which I am the invitee," he also recognizes the limitations of metaphors when speaking of God. None goes far enough in Greeley's opinion. In one of his prayers, Greeley talks with God about the inadequacy of his metaphors for God: "You are more vulnerable than the most vulnerable of human lovers, more obsessed

with us than any storyteller is with his characters, more in passionate love with us, to use the central metaphor, than any human lover could possibly be" (pp. 95, 107). See also Andrew M. Greeley, *Love Affair: A Prayer Journal* (New York: Cross-roads, 1992).

7. Ibid.

8. Robert Farrar Capon, *Hunting the Divine Fox: An Introduction to the Language of Theology* (New York: The Seabury Press, 1985), 41.

9. Ibid.

10. Sallie McFague, *Models of God: Theology for an Ecological, Nuclear Age* (Philadelphia: Fortress Press, 1987), 126.

11. Foster, *Prayer*, 3.

12. Ibid.

Chapter Two: Meaningful Prayer

1. John Killenger, *Prayer: The Act of Being with God* (Waco, Tex.: Word Books, 1981).

2. In the Pentateuch, God is addressed as El (strength or power), El Shaddai (God of the mountains or high places), El Elyon (the high God), El Olam (the God of eternity), El Berith (God of the covenant), and Adonai (Lord). But Yahweh (Jehovah) is by far the name most often used in speaking to God.

    The psalmist also spoke to God by means of a variety of names: "O Lord" (3:1), "O my God" (3:7), "O Lord my God" (7:1), "O Shepherd of Israel" (80:1), "Lord God of hosts" (80:4), "God of Jacob" (81:1), and "O Most High" (92:1).

    In the New Testament, the apostle Paul ascribed many titles to God in his prayers: "God of steadfastness and encour-agement" (Rom. 15:5), "God of hope" (Rom. 15:13), "God of peace" (Rom. 15:33), and "the only wise God" (Rom. 16:27). "God and Father of our Lord Jesus Christ," "Father of mer-cies," and "God of all comfort" (2 Cor. 1:3, RSV), "Father of glory" (Eph. 1:17), "King of ages, immortal, invisible, the only God" (1 Tim. 1:17).

3. The four Gospels in the New Testament relay some of the titles with which Jesus addressed God: "Our Father" (Matt. 6:9), "Father, Lord of heaven and earth" (Matt. 11:25), "My Father" (Matt. 26:39), "Abba, Father" (Mark 14:36), "Holy Father" (John 17:11), and "Righteous Father" (John 17:25).

Chapter Three: Imaging God

1. J. B. Phillips, *Your God Is Too Small* (New York: The Macmillan Company, 1960), 62.

2. Ibid., 38.

3. Roland H. Bainton, *Here I Stand: A Life of Martin Luther* (New York: Abingdon Press, 1950), 59.

4. Durwood L. Buchheim, *The Power of Darkness: Sermons for Lent and Easter* (Lima, Ohio: C. S. S. Publishing Company, Inc., 1985), 37.

5. John V. Taylor, *Weep Not for Me: Meditations on the Cross and the Resurrection* (Geneva: World Council of Churches, 1986), 8, quoting John Austin Baker from a book entitled, *The Foolishness of God.*

6. Quoted in Jurgen Moltmann, *The Crucified God* (New York: Harper & Row Publishers, 1974), 207.

7. Norman Pittenger wrote, "Very likely [Jesus] came to the conviction that only . . . through obedience to the point of death, could he disclose and impart the reality which evidently possessed him completely: the reality of God . . . as cosmic Lover, whose care for his people would go to any lengths and would accept suffering, anguish, even death, if this would bring to his children a full and abundant life . . . in and under his loving yet demanding care." *The Divine Triunity* (Philadelphia: United Church Press, 1977), 26, cited in McFague, *Models of God*, 215.

8. Meister Eckhart, ed. F. Pfeiffer, trans. C. de B. Evans (London: Watkins, 1924), 255, cited in Douglas V. Steere, "The Mystical Experience," *Review and Expositor* 71, no. 3, (1974): 328–29.

Chapter Four: Defining Love

1. Helen E. Fisher, *Anatomy of Love: The Natural History of Monogamy, Adultery, and Divorce* (New York: W. W. Norton and Company, 1992), 165.

2. Walter Eichrodt, *Theology of the Old Testament*, trans. J. A. Baker (Philadelphia: The Westminster Press, 1961), 252.

3. Interpretations of Plato's view of erotic love vary among scholars. However, most agree that Plato advocated a concentration on higher goals than those of giving and receiving love because he saw eros as a negative force. Yet, in Plato's mind, eros had

an upward pull about it, a force which caused a soul to yearn for a return to the divine realm. Plato's exploration of love in The Symposium provides one of the most ancient attempts to understand love that has survived. Examinations of Plato's thoughts on love can be found in Diane Ackerman, *A Natural History of Love* (New York: Random House, 1994), 95–99, and Joanne H. Stroud, *The Bonding of Will and Desire* (New York: Continuum, 1994), 25–26.

4. The writings of Dennis de Rougemont have significantly shaped intense and widespread criticisms of romantic love: *Love Declared: Essays on the Myths of Love* (New York: Pantheon Books, 1963) and *Love in the Western World*, trans. Montgomery Belgion (New York: Pantheon Books Inc., 1983). Though de Rougemont recognizes a tendency toward a pursuit of self-oriented pleasure in eros, he fails to acknowledge the potential power of eros to lead a person into authentic love.

5. The author of a twelfth-century volume entitled, *The Art of Courtly Love*, described love as "a certain inborn suffering derived from the right of an excessive meditation upon the beauty of the opposite sex." Andreas Capellanus, *The Art of Courtly Love*, trans. John Jay Parry (New York: Columbia University Press, 1941), 4.

6. Thomas Moore declares, "No matter how unrealistic in relation to the structures of life, no matter how illusory and dangerous, romantic love is as important to the soul as any other kind of love." *Soul Mates: Honoring the Mysteries of Love and Relationship* (New York: HarperCollins Publishers, 1994).

7. John Welwood, *Journey of the Heart: Intimate Relationship and the Path of Love* (New York: Harper Perennial, 1991), 60.

8. Prentiss L. Pemberton, *Dialogue in Romantic Love: Promise and Communication* (Valley Forge, Pa.: Judson Press, 1965), 14.

9. Stroud, *The Bonding of Will and Desire*, 25.

10. C. S. Lewis, *The Four Loves* (London: Collins Clear-Type Press, 1965), 88.

11. Anders Nygren, *Agape and Eros*, trans. Philip S. Watson (London: SPCK, 1957).

12. Gene Outka, "Love," *The Westminster Dictionary of Christian Ethics*, ed. James F. Childress and John Macquarrie (Philadelphia: The Westminster Press, 1986), 357.

13. Stroud, *The Bonding of Will and Desire*, 33.

14. James B. Nelson, *Embodiment: An Approach to Sexuality and Christian Theology* (Minneapolis: Augsburg Publishing House, 1978), 112.

15. Ibid., 113.

16. Nelson, *Embodiment*, 33.

17. Louise Cowan, "Introduction, Epic as Cosmopoesis," *The Epic Cosmos*, ed. Larry Allums (Dallas: Dallas Institute Publications, 1992), 24, cited in Stroud, *The Bonding of Will and Desire*, 19.

18. Augustine, *The Confessions of St. Augustine*, trans. Sir Tobie Matthew, rev. Dom Roger Hudleston (London: Collins Clear-Type Press, 1965), 31. In this older translation of Augustine's classic work, the well-known quotation appears in a more stilted form: "thou has created us for thyself, and our heart knows no rest, until it may repose in thee."

19. F. Forrester Church and Terrence J. Mulry, eds., *The Macmillan Book of Earliest Christian Prayers* (New York: Macmillan Publishing Company, 1988), 43.

20. Carol Lee Flinders, *Enduring Grace: Living Portraits of Seven Women Mystics* (HarperSanFrancisco, 1993), 88, and Richard J. Foster, *Prayer: Finding the Heart's True Home* (Harper SanFrancisco, 1992), 3.

21. Evelyn Underhill, *Mysticism: The Preeminent Study in the Nature and Development of Spiritual Consciousness* (New York: Doubleday, 1990), 87.

22. Ibid., 89.

23. Ibid., 85.

24. Welwood, *Journey of the Heart*, 65.

25. Martin E. Marty, *Friendship* (Allen, Tex.: Argus Communications, 1980), 125.

26. Eugene Kennedy, *On Being a Friend* (New York: Continuum, 1982), 113.

27. Gottfried Quell and Ethelbert Stauffer, "agapao, agape, agapetos," *Theological Dictionary of the New Testament*, ed. Gerhard Kittel, trans. Geoffrey W. Bromiley (Grand Rapids: Wm. B. Eerdmans Publishing Company, 1976), 1:128. Reflecting this agape-like understanding of philia, in the early 1100s, Aelred of Rievaulx wrote that he would not hesitate to say, "He who abides in friendship abides in God and God in him." Pauline

Matarasso, trans. and ed., *The Cistercian World: Monastic Writings of the Twelfth Century* (New York: Penguin Books, 1993), 143.

28. Marty compared friendship to love using four characteristics assigned to love by H. Richard Niebuhr, whom he called "a titan among modern Christian thinkers." Marty, *Friendship*, 126–31.

29. Ibid., 128.

30. Ibid., 131.

31. Gustav Stahlin, "*phileo, kataphileo, philema, philos, philo, philia,*" *Theological Dictionary of the New Testament*, 10:164.

32. Emil Brunner, *The Divine Imperative*, trans. Olive Wyon (Philadelphia: The Westminster Press, 1947), 517–18.

33. Lewis, *The Four Loves*, 72.

34. Sallie McFague, *Models of God: Theology for an Ecological, Nuclear Age* (Philadelphia: Fortress Press, 1988), 163.

35. Kennedy, *On Being a Friend*, 85.

36. Jean Massillon, "On Prayer," *Twenty Centuries of Great Preaching: An Encyclopedia of Preaching*, ed. Clyde E. Fant, Jr. and William M. Pinson, Jr. (Waco, Tex.: Word Books, 1971), 2:433.

37. Brunner, *The Divine Imperative*, 115.

38. Ibid., 55.

39. Lewis, *The Four Loves*, 7-14.

40. Moore, *Soul Mates*, 164.

Chapter Five: Loving God

1. Robert Farrar Capon, *The Third Peacock: The Problem of God and Evil* (Minneapolis: Winston Press, 1986), 21.

2. John Powell, *Why Am I Afraid to Love?* (Chicago: Argus Communications Co., 1967), 10.

3. John Powell, *Unconditional Love: Love Without Limits* (Allen, Tex.: Tabor Publishing, 1978), 92.

4. Thomas Moore, *Soul Mates: Honoring the Mysteries of Love and Relationship* (New York: Harper Collins Publishers, 1994), 23, and Patrick Thomas Malone and Thomas Patrick Malone, *The Windows of Experience, Moving Beyond Recovery to Wholeness* (New York: Simon & Schuster, 1992), 19.

5. Malone and Malone, *The Windows of Experience*, assert, "Intimacy without closeness, that is, pseudointimacy, is an escape. It bears no resemblance to the reality of love" (p. 231).

6. Thomas Patrick Malone and Patrick Thomas Malone, *The Art of Intimacy* (New York: Prentice Hall Press, 1987), 120.

7. John Welwood, *Journey of the Heart: Intimate Relationship and the Path of Love* (New York: Harper Perennial, 1991), 5.

8. Malone and Malone, *The Art of Intimacy*, 263.

9. Moore, *Soul Mates*, 115–16.

10. Malone and Malone, *The Windows of Experience*, 218, 225.

11. Malone and Malone, *The Art of Intimacy*, 29.

12. Ernest T. Campbell, *Locked in a Room with Open Doors* (Waco, Tex.: Word Books, 1974), 20, citing Hans Sachs, *Masks of Love and Life* (Cambridge, Mass.: Science-Art Publishers, 1948), 54.

13. Malone and Malone, *The Windows of Experience*, 202.

14. Welwood, *Journey of the Heart*, 88.

15. *Book of Common Worship: Daily Prayer* (Louisville, Ky.: Westminster/John Knox Press, 1993), 13.

Chapter Six: Praying Honestly

1. Frank Pittman, *Private Lies: Infidelity and the Betrayal of Intimacy* (New York: W.W. Norton & Company, 1989), 281.

2. Robert Van de Weyer, comp., *The HarperCollins Book of Prayers: A Treasury of Prayers Through the Ages* (Harper San Francisco, 1993), 221.

3. Augustine, *The Confessions of St. Augustine*, trans. Sir Tobie Matthew, rev. Dom Roger Hudleston (London: Collins Clear-Type Press, 1965), 100.

4. Thomas à Kempis, *The Imitation of Christ*, trans. Richard Whitford (New York: Washington Square Press, Inc., 1964), 7.

5. Thomas Merton, *Conjectures of a Guilty Bystander* (Garden City, N. Y.: Image Books, 1968), 70.

6. Philip Yancey, *Disappointment with God: Three Questions No One Asks Aloud* (Grand Rapids: Zondervan Publishing House, 1988), 149.

7. Weyer, *HarperCollins Book of Prayers*, 35.

8. Yancey, *Disappointment with God*, 93.

9. Weyer, *HarperCollins Book of Prayers*, 23.

10. Ibid., 215.

11. Dag Hammarskjöld, *Markings*, trans. Leif Sjoberg and W. H. Auden (New York: Alfred A. Knopf, 1981), 166.

12. Carol Lee Flinders, *Enduring Grace: Living Portraits of Seven Women Mystics* (Harper San Francisco, 1993), 144.

13. C. Welton Gaddy, *Prayers from Adoration to Zeal* (Valley Forge: Judson Press, 1993), 82.

14. Ibid., 82–83.

15. Horton Davies, ed., *The Communion of Saints: Prayers of the Famous* (Grand Rapids: William B. Eerdmans Publishing Company, 1990), 73.

16. Weyer, *HarperCollins Book of Prayers*, 209.

17. Henri J. M. Nouwen, *A Cry for Mercy: Prayers from the Genesee* (Garden City, N. Y.: Doubleday & Company, Inc., 1981), 70.

18. Weyer, *HarperCollins Book of Prayers*, 176–77.

19. Gaddy, *Prayers from Adoration to Zeal*, 28.

20. Weyer, *HarperCollins Book of Prayers*, 195.

21. Mary Wilder Tileston, *Prayers Ancient and Modern* (New York: Doubleday and McClure Co., 1897), 72.

22. Weyer, *HarperCollins Book of Prayers*, 395.

23. Ibid., 161.

24. Davies, *The Communion of Saints*, 112.

Chapter Seven: Praying Specifically

1. Elizabeth Barrett Browning, "Sonnets from the Portuguese," *Library of World Poetry: Being Choice Selections from the Best Poets*, ed. William Cullen Bryant (New York: Chatham River Press, 1970), 111.

2. William Temple, *Readings in St. John's Gospel* (London: Macmillan and Company, 1940), 68.

3. Mary Wilder Tileston, *Prayers Ancient and Modern* (New York: Doubleday and McClure Co., 1897), 17.

4. Daniel Berrigan, *Uncommon Prayer: A Book of Psalms* (New York: The Seabury Press, 1978), 26–27.

5. Walter Chalmers Smith, "Immortal, Invisible, God Only Wise," *The Baptist Hymnal*, ed. Wesley L. Forbis (Nashville: Convention Press, 1991), 6.

6. William Johnston, *Being in Love: The Practice of Christian Prayer* (London: HarperCollins Religious, 1989), 45.

7. C. Welton Gaddy, *The Gift of Worship* (Nashville: Broadman Press, 1992), 127.

8. Mary Wilder Tileston, *Prayers Ancient and Modern*, 32.

9. Pauline Matarasso, trans. and ed., *The Cistercian World: Monastic Writings of the Twelfth Century* (New York: Penguin Books, 1993), 195.

10. Carol Lee Flinders, *Enduring Grace: Living Portraits of Seven Women Mystics* (Harper San Francisco, 1993), 144.

11. J. P. Allen, "Prayer—Perspective from the Pulpit," *Southwestern Journal of Theology* 15, no. 2 (Spring 1972), 76–77.

12. Kathleen Norris, *Dakota: A Spiritual Geography* (New York: Ticknor & Fields, 1993), 188.

13. Henry J. M. Nouwen, *A Cry for Mercy: Prayers from the Genesee* (Garden City, N. Y.: Doubleday & Company, Inc., 1981), 116.

14. Joanne H. Stroud, *The Bonding of Will and Desire* (New York: Continuum, 1994), 79.

15. Johnson Oatman, Jr., "Count Your Blessings," *The Baptist Hymnal*, 644.

Chapter Eight: Praying Obediently

1. Henry C. Simmons, *In the Footsteps of the Mystics: A Guide to the Spiritual Classics* (New York: Paulist Press, 1992), 46.

2. Ibid.

3. Ibid., 41.

4. Catherine Marshall, ed., *The Prayers of Peter Marshall* (New York: McGraw-Hill Book Company, Inc., 1954), 99.

5. Ibid.

6. Donald P. McNeill, Douglas A. Morrison, and Henri J. M. Nouwen, *Compassion: A Reflection on the Christian Life* (Garden City, N. Y.: Image Books, 1983), 110.

7. Robert Van de Weyer, comp., *The HarperCollins Book of Prayers: A Treasury of Prayers Through the Ages* (Harper San Francisco, 1993), 287.

8. The same truth expressed in different words can be found in a prayer on enemies in C. Welton Gaddy, *Prayers from Adoration to Zeal* (Valley Forge, Pa.: Judson Press, 1993), 32.

9. Weyer, *The HarperCollins Book of Prayers*, 35.

10. Jan Ruysbroeck, *The Adornment of the Spiritual Marriage*, trans. C. A. W. Dom (London: Dent, 1916), 131, cited in Douglas V. Steere, "The Mystical Experience," *Review and Expositor*, 71, no. 3 (1974), 331.

11. George Fox, "Everyman," *Journal*, (New York: Dutton, 1948), 35, cited in Steere, "The Mystical Experience," 331.

12. F. Forrester Church and Terrence J. Mulry, eds., *The Macmillan Book of Earliest Christian Prayers* (New York: Macmillan Publishing Company, 1988), 39–40.

13. Theodore Parker Ferris, *Prayers* (New York: The Seabury Press, 1981), 59.

14. John Hunter, *Devotional Services* (E. P. Dutton & Co., Inc.) quoted in Paul S. McElroy, comp. and ed., *A Sourcebook for Christian Worship* (Cleveland: The World Publishing Company, 1968), 179.

15. Horton Davies, ed., *The Communion of Saints: Prayers of the Famous* (Grand Rapids: William B. Eerdmans Publishing Company, 1990), 85.

16. Ibid.

17. Weyer, *The HarperCollins Book of Prayers*, 21.

18. Davies, *The Communion of Saints*, 76.

19. Weyer, *The HarperCollins Book of Prayers*, 350.

20. Davies, *The Communion of Saints*, 20.

21. Foster, *Prayer*, 55.

22. For statements of this concept in the Bible, see 1 Corinthians 1:25; 3:18–19; and 4:10. For an elaboration of this concept as a trait of the Christian life, see C. Welton Gaddy, *God's Clowns: Messengers of the Good News* (San Francisco: Harper & Row, 1990). For an illustration of this truth in the life of a single individual, see Julien Green, *God's Fool: The Life and Times of Francis of Assisi*, trans. Peter Heinegg (San Francisco: Harper & Row, 1983).

Chapter Nine: Praying Persistently

1. Eduard Schweizer, *The Good News According to Matthew*, trans. David E. Green (Atlanta: John Knox Press, 1975), 173.

2. C. S. Lewis, *Letters to Malcolm: Chiefly on Prayer* (New York: Harcourt Brace Jovanovich, 1964), 113–15.

3. Scholars disagree over the exact origin of the "canonical hours." Whether Jewish observances of the third, sixth, and ninth hours as times of prayer or the Roman division of the day into four "hours" and the night into four "watches" gave rise to the canonical hours, no can say with certainty. Today people who observe canonical hours usually acknowledge a morning prayer (lauds), an evening prayer (vespers), a midday prayer (little hour), a night prayer (compline), and one prayer time which can be observed at any suitable point during a day. C. W. Dugmore, "Canonical Hours," *The New Westminster Dictionary of Liturgy and Worship*, ed. J. G. Davies (Philadelphia: The Westminster Press, 1986), 140–47.

4. Howard Thurman, *With Head and Heart: The Autobiography of Howard Thurman* (New York: Harcourt, Brace, Jovanovich, 1979), 122.

5. Arthur John Gossip, *The Galilean Accent: Being Some Studies in the Christian Life* (Edinburgh: T. & T. Clark, 1958), 277.

6. Robert J. McCracken, *Questions People Ask: Sermons Preached in Riverside Church*, New York City (New York: Harper & Brothers, 1951), 37.

7. Ibid., 42.

Chapter Ten: Praying Expectantly

1. Karl Barth, *Prayer*, 2d ed., trans. Sara F. Terrien, ed. Don E. Saliers (Philadelphia: The Westminster Press, 1985), 16.

2. Patrick D. Miller, *They Cried to the Lord: The Form and Theology of Biblical Prayer* (Minneapolis: Fortress Press, 1994), 226.

3. Robert G. Torbet, *A History of the Baptists*, rev. ed. (Valley Forge: The Judson Press, 1963), 81.

4. John Woolman, *The Journal of John Woolman and a Plea for the Poor*, The John Greenleaf Whittier Edition Text (Secaucus, N.J.: The Citadel Press, 1961), 85, 151.

5. Ibid., 186.

6. Ibid., 149.

7. Malcolm Muggeridge, *Something Beautiful for God: Mother Teresa of Calcutta* (Garden City, N.Y.: Image Books, 1977), 30.

8. Mother Teresa, *Words to Live By . . .* (Notre Dame, Ind.: Ave Maria Press, 1983), 23.

9. Ibid., 22.

10. Muggeridge, *Something Beautiful for God*, 39.

11. Teresa, *Words to Live By . . .* , 47.

12. Horton Davies, ed., *The Communion of Saints: Prayers of the Famous* (Grand Rapids: William B. Eerdmans Publishing Company, 1990), 101.

13. Jean-Nicholas Grou, *How to Pray*, trans. Joseph Dalby (Greenwood, S.C.: Attic, 1982), 82 cited in Richard J. Foster, *Prayer: Finding the Heart's True Home* (Harper San Francisco, 1992), 174.

14. Donald P. McNeill, Douglas A. Morrison, and Henri J. M. Nouwen, *Compassion: A Reflection on the Christian Life* (Garden City, N.Y.: Image Books, 1983), 109.

15. Ibid., 121.

16. Robert Van de Weyer, comp., *The HarperCollins Book of Prayers: A Treasury of Prayers Through the Ages* (HarperSanFrancisco, 1993), 51.

&